Scots E, , Dundee

1715 - 1835

David Dobson

CLEARFIELD

Copyright © 2024
by David Dobson
All Rights Reserved

Published for Clearfield Company by
Genealogical Publishing Company
Baltimore, Maryland
2024

ISBN: 9780806359700

Family historians seeking their Scottish origins before 1855, when statutory registration was introduced, have a major research source in the form of a massive database covering baptisms, marriages, and deaths as recorded in the Old Parish Registers of the Church of Scotland and the registers of the Roman Catholic Church. People of Episcopalian origin, however, have no such source at their disposal. While a handful of the Episcopalian registers, where they exist, have been published, the majority are in manuscript form and are scattered throughout the country in churches and archives.

In 1689 Presbyterianism became the established form of church government in Scotland and those people who wished to retain Episcopacy withdrew from the parish churches to form their own congregations. The Episcopalians were generally in favour of the House of Stuart and the Jacobite Cause, which led to Penal Laws being introduced from 1712. As a result, two distinct Episcopalian churches developed: the Qualified Episcopal Church, which prayed for the Hanoverian monarchs, used the English liturgy and prayer book, and employed Anglican clergy; and the other, which was under severe restrictions and retained the Scottish Episcopal practices.

In Dundee both churches existed and retained their independence until the early nineteenth century. The existence of records of baptisms, marriages, and deaths for Episcopalians are virtually non-existent in Dundee until around 1810. To identify who were members of the churches it has been necessary to use other sources, such as the vestry records and financial records, where available. The outcome of that effort is this partial compilation, which cites many, though not all, members of the church during the period 1715 to 1835. It is clear from the data in this book that most members were from Dundee and surrounding counties, but there were a substantial number from England and Ireland, as well as a handful from Germany and the Netherlands. A number of these Episcopalians had family links to Jamaica and India. This book is designed as an aid to genealogists and historians and is overwhelmingly based on records in St. Paul's Cathedral and in the Dundee City Archives.

David Dobson
Dundee, Scotland, 2024

DCA	=	Dundee City Archives ms
		Vestry Minute Books
		Cash Books
E/QEC	=	English or Qualified Episcopal Chapel, Dundee, ms
		Baptismal Register
		Marriage Register
ECD	=	'Historical Account of the Settlement of the Episcopal Congregation in Dundee in 1727', [Dundee, 1744]
F	=	Fasti
S	=	Scottish Episcopal Church, Dundee, ms
		Baptismal Register
		Marriage Register
SEC	=	Scottish Episcopal Clergy, 1689-2000, D M Bertie, Edinburgh, 2000

Abbreviations

[E]	=	English Chapel
QEC	=	Qualified Episcopal Chapel
[S]	=	Scottish Church

St. Paul's Scottish Episcopal Cathedral, Dundee

Castle Street Church, around 1800

ABBOT, ALEXANDER, bapt. 1825, 1st son of William Abbot, a labourer, born in Dundee, and his wife Elizabeth, 2nd dau. of William Read, a labourer in Murroes, Angus. [E]

ABBOT, ANN CROCKATT, born 9 June 1821, bapt.24 June 1821, 2nd dau. of William Abbot, a labourer born in Dundee, and his wife Elizabeth, dau. of William Read, a labourer in Murroes, Angus. [E]

ABBOT, BETSEY, born 11 May, bapt., 30 May 1824, 4th dau. of William Abbot, a labourer born in Dundee, and his wife Elizabeth, dau. of William Read, a labourer in Murroes, Angus. [E]

ABBOT, DAVID, in Dundee, 1727. [ECD]

ABBOT, WILLIAM, pensioner, 1743. [DCA.GD/EC/D10/2/1]

ABBOT, CHRISTIAN, born 7 Nov., bapt. 24 Nov.1822, 3rd dau. of William Abbot, a labourer born in Dundee, and his wife Elizabeth, dau. of William Read, a labourer in Murroes, Angus. [E]

ABBOT, ISABELLA, born 21 Dec.1819, bapt. 9 Jan.1820, first dau. of William Abbot, a labourer born in Dundee, and his wife Elizabeth, dau. of William Read, a labourer in Murroes, Angus. [E]

ADAM, CHARLES, vestryman, 1802. [DCA.GD/EC/D10/1/2][S]

ADAM, DAVID, son of Charles Adam and his wife Euphemia, born 13 Feb., bapt. 19 Mar. 1816. [S]

ADAM, MARGARET, pensioner, 1740. [DCA.GD/EC/DIO/2/1]

ADAM, STUART, dau. (sic) of James Adam and Elizabeth Robinson, born 12 Aug., bap. 13 Oct. 1816. [S]

ADAM, Mrs, a member of the Scots Episcopal Chapel, Castle Street, Dundee 1824. [GD.EC.D1 0.1/3]

ADAMS, A., 1829. [GD.EC.D10.1/3]

ADAMS, MARGARET, born 20 June, bapt. 29 June 1817, dau. of Alexander Adams, a hatter, born in Drumachose, County Londonderry, Ireland, and his wife Rose, dau. of John McIlheran, a tailor in Ballymena, County Antrim, Ireland. [E]

ADAMSON, ISABEL, a pensioner aged 70 in 1818. [S] [DCA.GD.EC.D10.1/2]

ADAMSON, JOHN, born 20 Sep. bapt. 22 Oct. 1820, first son of John Adamson, a nailer born in Dundee, and his wife Janet, dau. of David Campbell in Dundee. [E]

ADAMSON, PETER, born 28 Sep. bapt. 7 Oct. 1827, 5th son of John Adamson, a nailer born in Dundee, and his wife Janet, dau. of David Campbell a labourer in Airlie, Angus. [E]

ADAMSON, MARGARET, dau of John Adamson and Anne Hunter, born in May, bapt. 3 Sept 1811. [S]

ADDISON, Miss E., a member of the Scots Episcopal Chapel, Castle Street, Dundee, 1824. [DCA.GD.EC.D10.1/3]

ADDISON, WILLIAM, beadle, 1816/1817/1818. [S] [DARC.GD.EC.D10.1/2]

ADIE, MARY ANDERSON, 3rd dau of John Adie weaver, born in Glasgow, and his wife Ann, dau of Charles Flannagan, born in Kilworth, County Cork, Ireland, born 2 July, bapt. 2 July 1809. [E]

ADIE, P., session clerk, 1812. [E]

AIKIN, ROBERT, born 29 Aug., bapt. 8 Oct. 1820, first son of James Aikin, a sailor born in Denny, Stirlingshire, and his wife Elizabeth, dau. of David Watt a brass-founder in Alloa, Stirlingshire. [E]

AIRD, JANE, dau of John Aird and Mary his wife, born 25 July, bapt. 9 Aug. 1812. [S]

AIRTH, JOHN, a smith, church member, 1777. [DCA:GD/EC/D10/1/2][S]

AITKEN, JAMES, a bachelor in Dundee, and Jean Ayton, a spinster in Dundee, were married in the vestry of St Paul's, Dundee, 21 Oct. 1832. [S]

ALEXANDER, ELEANOR, 1st dau of George Alexander labourer, born in Aberlinley, and his wife Isabella, dau of Alexander Crichton weaver in Arbroath, Angus, born 3 Dec, bapt. 7 Dec 1809. [E]

ALEXANDER, JAMES, and his five sisters, church members, 1764. [DCA.GD/EC/DIO/2/1]

ALEXANDER, JANE, a spinster in Dundee, and George Brunton, a bachelor in St Mary's parish, Edinburgh, married in her father's house in Murraygait, Dundee, 1 Oct. 1827. [S]

ALEXANDER, JOHN, church member, 1781. [DCA.GD/EC/D10/1/2][S]

ALEXANDER, MARY, dau. of George Alexander and his wife Mary, born 11 Dec. 1815, bap. 14 Jan. 1816. [S]

ALISON, BELL, church member, 1746. [DCA.GD/EC/D10/2/1]

ALISON, ROBERT, a bachelor, and Elizabeth Laird, both in Dundee, were married on 17 Sept. 1815; witnesses were ....Scott and John Alison. [S]

ALISON, ROBERT, son of Robert Alison and Elizabeth his wife, born 7 July, bapt. 27 July 1816. [S]

ALISON, WILLIAM, and his wife, members of the Scots Episcopal Chapel, Castle Street, Dundee, 1824. [DCA.GD.EC.D10.1/3]

ALLEN, ANNE, dau of John Allen and Ellen Smith, born 28 Jan. bapt. 19 June 1814. [S]

ALLAN, ELIZABETH TATE, born 22 July, bapt. 25 Aug. 1816, dau. of John Allan, a mason, born in Dundee, and his wife Mary Fell, dau. of Ann Bristow in Keswick, Cumberland, England. [E]

ALLAN, ELIZABETH, born 12 Sep., bapt. 13 Sep. 1820, first dau. of Richard Allan, born in Clunis, County Monaghan, Ireland, a Private of the 8th Royal Veteran Battalion, and his wife Jane, dau. of Alexander Jackson, a carpenter in Killyshendry, County Cavan, Ireland. [E]

ALLAN, JOHN, of Strathmartin, Angus, 1785. [DCA.GD/EC/D10/2/2][E]

ALLAN, JOHN, mason, and Margaret Fell, both in Dundee, were married 21 Nov.1813. [E]

ALLAN, RICHARD WARREN, 1st son of John Allan mason, born in Dundee, and his wife Mary Fell, dau. of Ann Bristow a single-woman in Keswick, Cumberland, England, born 2 Dec. bapt. 26 Dec. 1814. [E]

ANDERSON, ALEXANDER, son of William Anderson and Jane his wife, born 12 Jan. bapt. 29 Jan 1815. [S]

ANDERSON, ANNY, dau. of John Anderson and Catherine his wife, born 13 July, bapt. 19 July 1813. [S]

ANDERSON, AGNES, dau. of William Anderson and Jane his wife, born 7 Sep. bapt. 15 Sep. 1816. [S]

ANDERSON, ANN, born 4 Aug. bapt. 20 Sep. 1818, first dau. of William Anderson, a stocking weaver, born in Kilrenny, Fife, and his wife Isabella, dau. of James Adie, a shoemaker in Dundee. [E]

ANDERSON, DAVID, son of Andrew Anderson and Jane his wife, born 23 July, bapt. 28 July 1816. [S]

ANDERSON, DAVID, born 22 July, bapt. 3 Aug. 1823, 1st son of David Anderson, a groom, born in Dundee, and his wife Jane, dau. of the late John Fraser, a Private soldier of the 42nd Regiment of Foot. [E]

ANDERSON, DAVID, a member of the Scots Episcopal Chapel, Castle Street, Dundee, 1824; a vestryman, 1833. [DCA.GD.EC.D10.1/3]

ANDERSON, DAVID, a bachelor in Dundee, and Martha Bain, a spinster in Dundee, were married in the house of William Butchart, a mason in Forebank, Dundee, 19 Apl. 1826. [S]

ANDERSON, ELIZABETH BRUCE, born 1 Jan., bapt. 11 Jan. 1824, 4th dau. of William Anderson, born in Meigle, Perthshire, an innkeeper in Peter Street, Dundee, and his wife Jane, dau. of James Boddo, a slater in Dundee. [E]

ANDERSON, ELIZABETH, a spinster in Dundee, and Sir William Scott of Ancrum, Roxburghshire, a bachelor, were married in the house of Mrs Anderson, Balgay, Dundee, 9 June 1828. [S]

ANDERSON, GEORGE, church member, 1784. [DCA.GD/EC/D10/2/2][E]

ANDERSON, GEORGE, son of David Anderson and Isabel Barron, born 11 Dec. 1812, bapt. 6 Feb. 1814. [S]

ANDERSON, HELEN, born 15 Apr., bapt. 13 May 1827, 3rd dau. of James Anderson, a blacksmith, born in Dundee, and his wife Elizabeth, dau. of Donald Mackenzie a porter in Dundee. [E]

ANDERSON, JAMES, a weaver, church member, 1777. [DCA:GD/EC/D10/1/2] [S]

ANDERSON, JAMES, 1st son of William Anderson stocking weaver, born in Kilrenny, Fife, and his wife Isabella, dau of James Adie, a shoemaker in Dundee, born 20 Nov. 1811, bapt. 20 Sept. 1818. [E]

ANDERSON, JAMES, son of John Anderson and Catherine his wife, born 1 Oct. bapt. 30 Oct. 1814. [S]

ANDERSON, JAMES, son of John Anderson and Catherine his wife, born 13 July, bapt. 19 July 1813. [S]

ANDERSON, JANE MAXWELL DOUGLAS, born 26 Dec., bapt. 31 Dec. 1826, 1st dau. of Andrew Anderson, a seaman, born in Dundee, and his wife Mary, dau. of Peter Cook a weaver in Dundee. [E]

ANDERSON, JOHN, a weaver, church member, 1777. [DCA.GD/EC/D10/1/2] [S]

ANDERSON, JOHN, a bachelor in Dundee, and Isabell Milne, a spinster in Dundee, were married in the house of Rev. Heneage Horsley, Magdalene Yard, Dundee, 2 Apl. 1834. [S]

ANDERSON, JOHN HETHERTON, born 7 Feb., bapt.13 Feb.1825, 1st son of Andrew Anderson, a seaman, born in Dundee, and his wife Mary, dau. of Peter Cook, a weaver in Dundee. [E]

ANDERSON, MARGARET, dau. of John Anderson and Catherine his wife, born 9 Apl., bapt. 28 Apl. 1816. [S]

ANDERSON, Miss MARY, a member of the Scots Episcopal Chapel, Castle Street, Dundee, 1824. [DCA.GD.EC.D10.1/3]

ANDERSON, MARY GRAHAM, born 24 Apr., bapt.17 May 1829, 2nd dau. of Andrew Anderson, a seaman, born in Dundee, and his wife Mary, dau. of Peter Cook, a weaver in Dundee. [E]

ANDERSON, THOMAS, a member of the Scots Episcopal Chapel, Castle Street, Dundee, 1824. [DCA.GD.EC.D10.1/3]

ANDERSON, WILLIAM, a weaver, church member, 1777. [DCA:GD/EC/D10/1/2] [S]

ANDERSON, WILLIAM, son of William Anderson and his wife Elizabeth, born 6 June, bapt. 14 July 1816. [S]

ANDERSON, WILLIAM, born 13 Sep., bapt. 24 Sep. 1826, 2nd son of David Anderson, a groom, born in Dundee, and his wife Jane, dau. of the late John Fraser, a Private soldier of the 42nd Regiment of Foot. [E]

ANDERSON, ..., member of QEC, 1776. [DCA:GD/EC/D10]

ANDERSON, ..., of Baldovie, Angus, a church member in 1784. [DCA.GD/EC/D10/2/2][E]

ANDREWS, WILLIAM, minister of the Qualified Chapel in Dundee, from 1807 to 1808. [DCA:GD/EC/D10]

ARBUTHNOTT, Dr ALEXANDER, in Dundee, 1727. [ECD]

ARCHER, ELIZABETH, a spinster in Kettins, Angus, married Daniel Henderson, a bachelor in Kettins, at the Toll House of Auchterhouse, Angus, 12 June 1819. [S]

ARCHIBALD, ANNA, dau. of William Archibald and Anna his wife, born 2 Dec. bapt. 10 Dec 1815. [S]

ARCHIBALD, MARY, dau. of John Archibald and Jane Thomson, born 12 July, bapt. 11 Sept 1814. [S]

ARMSTRONG, JANET, born 14 Mar., bapt. 21 Mar 1821, 1st son of Christopher Armstrong, a pensioner of the 8th Royal Veteran Battalion, born in Materculmane, County Fermanagh, Ireland, and his wife Susannah, dau. of Christopher Armstrong a farmer in Tiberet, County Fermanagh, Ireland. [E]

ARMSTRONG, JOHN, born 6 Dec., bapt. 15 Dec. 1816, son of James Armstrong, groom at Belmont, Perthshire, born in Coldstream, Berwickshire, and his wife Elizabeth Nicholson, dau. of John Nicholson, a cabinet maker in Cupar, Fife. [E]

AUCHENLECK, DAVID, in Dundee, 1727. [ECD]

AUCHENLECK, GILBERT, of that Ilk, in Angus in 1743. [DCA.GD/EC/DIO/2/1; 2/3]

AUCHENLECK, JOHN, church member, 1758, 1764. [DCA.GD/EC/DIO/2/1] [DCA.GD/EC/D10/2/2][E]

AUSTEN, DAVID BRYSON, born 28 June, bapt. 4 July 1821, 2nd son of John Austen, a jeweller, born in Madras, India, and his wife Jane, dau. of the late David Bryson, a manufacturer in Glasgow. [E]

AYTON, JEAN, a spinster in Dundee, and James Aitken, a bachelor in Dundee, were married in the vestry of St Paul's, Dundee, 21 Oct. 1832. [S]

BACHELOR, WILLIAM, born 16 Oct. 1822, bapt. 3 Jan. 1823, 2nd son of Thomas Bachelor, a printer, born in Birmingham, Warwickshire, England,

and his wife Priscilla, dau. of Francis Bachelor, a baker in Kynton, Warwickshire. [E]

BAILLIE, JOHN, a mason, church member, 1810. [DCA.GD/EC/D10/1/2] [S]

BAILLIE, JOHN, a bachelor in Dundee, and Clementina Ogilvy, a spinster in Dundee, were married in the vestry of St Paul's, Castle Street, Dundee, on 13 Nov. 1828. [S]

BAILLIE, MARIANNE, born 29 Mar., bapt. 25 Apr. 1824, 2nd dau. of David Baillie, a sawyer, born in Brechin, Angus, and his wife Isabella, dau. of James Williamson, a weaver in Aberdeen. [E]

BAILLIE, Mrs, a member of the Scots Episcopal Chapel, Castle Street, Dundee, 1824. [DCA.GD.EC.D10.1/3]

BAIN, HELEN, a pensioner, 1739. [DCA.GD/EC/DIO/2/1]

BAIN, MARTHA, a spinster in Dundee, and David Anderson, a bachelor in Dundee, were married in the house of William Butchart, a mason in Forebank, Dundee, 19 Apl. 1826. [S]

BAKER, GEORGE, a sailor, and Elizabeth Lawrence, both in Dundee, were married 12 Sep. 1819. [E]

BALENDEN, JAMES, a church member, 1781. [DCA.GD/EC/D10/1/2] [S]

BALFOUR, JOHN, son of …….. Balfour the younger of Forret, in Fife, was bapt. 5 June 1723. [BN]

BALL, ROBERT, born 12 Feb., bapt. 25 Feb. 1821, 1st son of William Ball, a drummer in the 8th Royal Veteran Battalion, born in Shipton Mallet, Somerset, England, and his wife Ann, dau. of Robert Mills, a Private in the same regiment. [E]

BALL, WILLIAM JOHN, born 4 Dec., bapt. 22 Dec. 1822, 2nd son of William Ball, a weaver, formerly a drummer in the 8th Royal Veteran Battalion, born in Shipton Mallet, Somerset, England, and his wife Ann, dau. of Robert Mills a Private in the same regiment. [E]

BALLINGALL, JAMES, a church member, 1784. [DCA.GD/EC/D10/2/2][E]

BALLINTINE, JAMES, a church member, 1743. [DCA.GD/EC/DIO/2/1; 2/3]

BALLANTINE, MARGARET, born 1 June, bapt.21 June 1829, 1st dau. of Walter Ballantine, a shoemaker, born in Duddingston, Midlothian, and his wife Margaret, dau. of John Dalrymple, a merchant in Fraserburgh, Aberdeenshire. [E]

BALMAIN, JAMES, a candle-maker, and Ann Bowman, both in Dundee, were married 15 June 1823. [E]

BALSKELLY, Lady, and her two sisters, church members, 1764. [DCA.GD/EC/DIO/2/1]

BANDENE, ISOBEL, a pensioner, 1740. [DCA.GD/EC/DIO/2/1]

BARNET, GRISSELL, a pensioner, 1739. [DCA.GD/EC/DIO/2/1]

BARRY, BETTY, dau of David Barry and Jane his wife, born 3 Oct, bapt. 15 Oct 1815. [S]

BARRY, JOHN, son of Thomas Barry and Elizabeth his wife, born 20 July, bapt. 11 Aug. 1816. [S]

BATHIE, ELIZABETH, a member of the QEC, 1776. [DCA:GD/EC/D10]

BATTHY, MARY, 11th dau of Andrew Batthy, a labourer, born in Dundee, and his wife Helen, dau of Thomas Laird, a weaver, born in Kirriemuir, Angus, born 20 June, bapt. 28 June 1811. [E]

BATTHY, WILLIAM GORDON, 2nd son of Andrew Batthy labourer, born in Dundee, and his wife Helen, dau. of Thomas Laird, a weaver, born in Kirriemuir, Angus, born 22 Feb, bapt. 5 Mar. 1809. [E]

BAUMBACH, GEORGE JOHN, a bachelor and a miner in Dundee, and Jane Cruickshank, a spinster in Arbroath, were married at the house of Miss Menzies in Dundee, 13 Jan. 1822. [S]

BAUMBACH, Mrs, a member of the Scots Episcopal Chapel, Castle Street, Dundee,1824. [DCA.GD.EC.D10.1/3]

BAXTER, GORDON, son of George Baxter and Hannah Wallis his wife, born 1 May, bapt. 13 June 1813. [S]

BAXTER, PETER or PATRICK, a church member, 1743. [DCA.GD/EC/DIO/2/1; 2/3]

BAXTER, THOMAS, son of Alexander Baxter and Jane his wife, born 9 Sept bapt. 12 Nov 1815. [S]

BAYNE, ANDERSON, born 17 Apr., bapt. 8 May 1823, 5th dau. of Charles Bayne, a teacher of dancing, born in Perth, and his wife Susan, dau. of Samuel Kyd, a farmer in Glenskenno. [E]

BAYNE, CHARLES, a church member, 1811. [DCA:GD/EC/D10]

BAYNE, CHARLES, born 7 May., bapt. 13 May 1821, 5th son of Charles Bayne, a teacher of dancing born in Perth, and his wife Susan, dau. of Samuel Kyd, a farmer in Glenskenno. [E]

BAYNE, DAVID MANSON, 3rd son of Charles Bayne, a teacher of dancing born in Perth, and his wife Susan, dau. of Samuel Kyd, a farmer in Glenskenno, Perthshire, born 19 Apr., bapt. 1 May 1813. [E]

BAYNE, ISABELLA ANDERSON, 2nd dau of Charles Bayne teacher of dancing, born in Perth, and his wife Susan, dau. of Samuel Kyd, a farmer in Glenskenno, Perthshire, born 23 Jan, bapt. 31 Jan 1810. [E]

BAYNE, JANET, dau. of William Bayne and Euphemia Laing, born 12 Feb, bapt. 15 Aug 1815. [S]

BAYNE, JANET, born 26 Jan., bapt. 10 Feb. 1819, 4th dau. of Charles Bayne, a teacher of dancing, born in Perth, and his wife Susan, dau. of Samuel Kyd, a farmer in Glenskenno. [E]

BAYNE, MARY, born 14 Feb., bapt. 5 Mar. 1817, dau. of Charles Bayne, a teacher of dancing, born in Perth, and his wife Susan, dau. of Samuel Kyd, a farmer in Glenskenno. [E]

BAYNE, PETER, 2nd son of Charles Bayne, teacher of dancing, born in Perth, and his wife Susan, dau. of Samuel Kyd, a farmer in Glenskenno born 19 Sept. bapt. 8 Oct 1811. [E]

BEARD, Mrs, member of the QEC, 1776. [DCA:GD/EC/D10]

BEARTIE, CATHERINE, dau. of David Beartie and Agnes Beartie, born 9 July, bapt. 14 Aug. 1814. [S]

BEATON, ..., of Balfour, Fife, in Dundee, 1727. [ECD]

BEATSON, ROBERT, a merchant in Dundee, QEC committee member, 1757. [DCA:GD/EC/D10] [DCA.GD/EC/D10/2/2][E]

BEATTIE, ANNE, dau of John Beattie and Margaret his wife, born 8 Dec, bapt. 19 Dec 1813. [S]

BEATTIE, DAVID, a member of the Scots Episcopal Chapel, Castle Street, Dundee, 1824; a vestryman, 1835. [DCA.GD.EC.D10.1/3]

BEATTIE, EUPHEMIA, a spinster in Dundee, married Ebenezer Stephen, a mason in Dundee, a bachelor, at the house of Andrew Hood, a vintner in St Clement's Lane, Dundee, on 9 May 1819.

BEATTIE, HENRY, in Dundee, 1727. [ECD]

BEATTIE, JOHN, son of John Beattie and Margaret his wife, born 23 Jan, bapt. 2 Feb 1812. [S]

BEATTIE, WILLIAM, son of John Beattie and Margaret his wife, born 6 Dec. bapt. 17 Dec. 1815. [S]

BEG, ELIZABETH, born 25 Feb., bapt. 11 Mar.1827, 1st dau. of James Beg a weaver, born in Dundee, and his wife Margaret, dau. of John Cameron, a nailer in Dundee. [E]

BEGBIE, Mrs, a member of the Scots Episcopal Chapel, Castle Street, Dundee, 1824. [DCA.GD.EC.D10.1/3]

BELL, ELIZABETH DARE, born 19 Jan., bapt. 15 Feb. 1829, 1st dau. of Robert Bell, an overseer in a spinning mill, born in Artrae, County Londonderry, Ireland, and his wife Colville, dau. of David Miller, a sawyer in Dundee. [E]

BELL, GEORGE, son of George Bell and Christian Chisholm, born 19 Apr. 1813, bapt. 9 Jan 1814. [S]

BELL, Mrs JOHN, a member of the QEC, 1776, 1784. [DCA:GD/EC/D10] [DCA.GD/EC/D10/2/2][E]

BELL, JOHN KEITH, son of Charles Bell and Andrina his wife, born 28 Aug., bapt. 20 Oct. 1816. [S]

BELL, MARY ANN, a spinster in Dundee, and John Ramsay, a widower in Dundee, were married in St Paul's, Castle Street, Dundee, 4 July 1830. [S]

BENNET, DAVID, 2nd son of William Bennet inn-keeper, born in Dundee, and his wife Ann, dau. of Ebenezer Oswald in Kirkcaldy, Fife, born 10 Sept, bapt. 22 Sept. 1811. [E]

BENNET, JOHN, 1829. [DCA.GD.EC.D10.1/3]

BENNY, ANDREW, church member, 1764. [DCA.GD/EC/DIO/2/1]

BERG, HERMINE HINNICHE, dau. of Herman Hinniche Berg and Mitta his wife, [from Germany?] born 20 Apr. bapt. 18 May 1813. [S]

BERRY, JAMES, in St Andrews, Fife, and Janet Black, in Leuchars, Fife, were married in the vestry of St Paul's, Castle Street, Dundee, 2 Aug. 1833. [S]

BESTUM {?}, DAVID, son of William Bestum and Margaret his wife, born 24 Aug bapt. 30 Aug 1812. [S]

BEUGIE, CHRISTIAN, a widow in Dundee, married James Gauld, a blacksmith in Dundee, 13 June 1823. [S]

BEVERLEY, MARGARET, dau of James Beverley and Isabel his wife, born 26 Apr. bapt. 18 May 1812. [S]

BEWICK, JAMES, born 27 July, bapt. 8 Aug. 1819, 4th son of Martin Bewick, a labourer, born in Gosforth, Northumberland, England, and his wife Jane, dau. of William Peter, a stone mason in Dundee. [E]

BEWICK, MARGARET, dau. of William Bewick and Sophia Johnson, born 29 Aug. bapt 12 Sept 1813. [S]

BEWICK, MARY, born 27 June, bapt. 13 July 1828, 2nd dau. of Martin Bewick, a labourer, born in Gosforth, Northumberland, England, and his wife Jane, dau. of William Peter, a stone mason in Dundee. [E]

BEWICK, PETER, born 7 Nov., bapt. 16 Nov. 1817, 3rd son of Martin Bewick, a labourer, born in Gosforth, Northumberland, England, and his s Jane, dau. of William Peter, a stone mason in Dundee. [E]

BEWICK, ROBERT DOIG, born 17 Jan., bapt. 27 Jan. 1826, 6th son of Martin Bewick, a labourer, born in Gosforth, Northumberland, England and his wife Jane, dau. of William Peter, a stone mason in Dundee. [E]

BIGGS, JANET, 1st dau. of Robert Biggs, a Private in the 2nd Battalion of the 79th Regiment of Foot, born in Wick, Calthness, and his wife Ann, dau. of John Donaldson, farmer in Alloa, Clackmannanshire, born 3 Jan. bapt 6 Jan 1811. [E]

BIGGING, JAMES, a member of the Scots Episcopal Chapel, Castle Street, Dundee, 1824. [DCA.GD.EC.D10.1/3]

BIRD, SARAH ANN, born 28 Dec. bapt. 31 Dec.1820, third dau. of James Bird, born in Birmingham, Warwickshire, England, a drummer of the 8th

Veteran Battalion, and his wife Esther, dau. of James Walls of Florence Court, Inniskilling, County Fermanagh, Ireland. [E]

BIRNIE, Miss ANN, a member of the Scots Episcopal Chapel, Castle Street, Dundee, 1824. [DCA.GD.EC.D10.1/3]

BIRNIE, Miss FLORA, a member of the Scots Episcopal Chapel, Castle Street, Dundee, 1824. [DCA.GD.EC.D10.1/3]

BIRNIE, G., and his wife, members of the Scots Episcopal Chapel, Castle Street, Dundee, 1824. [DCA.GD.EC.D10.1/3]

BIRNIE, GRAHAM (sic), a spinster in Dundee, and Thomas Mitchell, a bachelor in Dundee, were married in the vestry of St Paul's, Castle Street, Dundee, 17 June 1831. [S]

BISHOP, ANNE, dau. of George Bishop and Betty Dawson, born 1807, bapt. 1 Aug 1811. [S]

BISSET, DANIEL, of the local militia, and Margaret Nucator, both in Dundee, were married, 20 Nov 1809. [E]

BISSET, JAMES, church member, 1811. [DCA:GD/EC/D10]

BISSET, JAMES JACKSON, born 23 Sep., bapt. 21 Oct. 1827, dau. of Janet Bisset, dau. of the late James Bisset, a baker in Broughty Ferry, Angus. [E]

BISSET, JAMES, 3rd son of James Bisset, a baker in Nethergait, Dundee, born in Liff, Angus, and his wife Ann, dau. of Thomas Brewer, a labourer, born in Islington, Devon, England, born 22 June, bapt. 1 July 1810. [E]

BISSET, JANET, 3rd dau of James Bisset, a baker in the Nethergait, Dundee, born in Liff, Angus, and his wife Ann, dau. of Thomas Brewer, a labourer born in Islington, Devon, England, born 28 July, bapt. 4 Sept. 1808. [E]

BISSET, JANET KILGOUR, born 28 Sep. bapt. 8 Oct. 1820, 1st dau. of James Bisset, a butcher, born in Dundee, and his wife Catharine, dau. of the late James Bisset, a butcher in Dundee. [E]

BISSET, JOHN, pensioner, 1740. [DCA.GD/EC/DIO/2/1]

BISSET, LOUISA, and MARY THORBURN BISSET, born 6 Mar. bap. 1 June 1823, twin daus. of James Bisset, a butcher, born in Dundee, and his wife Catharine, dau. of the late James Bisset, a butcher in Dundee. [E]

BISSET, MARY, 4th dau. of James Bisset, a baker in the Nethergait, Dundee, born in Liff, Angus, and his wife Ann, dau. of Thomas Brewer, a labourer, born in Islington, Devon, England, born 16 Oct, bapt. 25 Oct 1812. [E]

BLACK, CATHARINE, born 10 Sep. 1827, bapt. 25 Sep. 1829, 1st dau. of James Black, a cattle dealer in Maxwelltown, Dundee, born in Tannadice, Angus, and his wife Mary, dau. of Charles Key, an inn-keeper in Brechin, Angus. [E]

BLACK, JAMES, a cattle-dealer, and Mary Kay, both in Dundee, were married, 25 Sep.1829. [E]

BLACK, JANET, born 31 Aug., bapt. 25 Sep. 1829, 1st dau. of James Black, a cattle dealer in Maxwelltown, Dundee, born in Tannadice, Angus, and his wife Mary, dau. of Charles Key, an inn-keeper in Brechin, Angus. [E]

BLACK, JANET, in Leuchars, Fife, and James Berry, in St Andrews, Fife, were married in the vestry of St Paul's, Castle Street, Dundee, 2 Aug. 1833. [S]

BLACK, JOHN, an Excise officer in Dundee, member QEC, 1810. [DCA.GD/EC/D10/1/2]

BLACK, JOHN, and his wife, members of the Scots Episcopal Chapel, Castle Street, Dundee, 1824/1828; a vestryman, 1833. [DCA.GD.EC.D10.1/3]

BLAIKIE, FRANCIS, a schoolmaster, church member, 1777. [DCA:GD/EC/D10/1/2][S]

BLAIR, DAVID, junior, a vestryman, 1823. [E][DCA.GD.EC.D10.1/1]

BLAIR, GEORGE, church member, 1777, 1781. [DCA:GD/EC/D10/1/2][S]

BLAIR, JOHN, pensioner, 1739. [DCA.GD/EC/DIO/2/1]

BLAIR, Captain, church member, 1811. [DCA:GD/EC/D10]

BLAKEY, MARGARET, a spinster in Dundee, and Samuel Johnson, a bachelor in Islington, Middlesex, were married in St Paul's, Castle Street, Dundee, 2 Mar. 1830. [S]

BLAKEY, Miss, a vestryman, St Paul's, Dundee, 1835. [DCA.GD.EC.D10.]

BLYTH, JOHN, church member, 1758. [DCA.GD/EC/D10/2/2][E]

BONNER, AGNES, born 14 Mar., bap. 5 Apl. 1818, dau. of Thomas Bonner, a painter born in Edinburgh, and his wife Mary, dau. of John Macdonald, a chairmaker in Edinburgh. [E]

BONNER, Miss ANN, a member of the Scots Episcopal Chapel, Castle Street, Dundee, 1824. [DCA.GD.EC.D10.1/3]

BONNER, ANNE, a spinster in Dundee, and James Beaton, a bachelor in Dundee, were married in the vestry of St Paul's, Castle Street, Dundee, 13 Aug. 1826. [S]

BONNER, Miss JEAN, a member of the Scots Episcopal Chapel, Castle Street, Dundee, 1824. [DCA.GD.EC.D10.1/3]

BONNER, JEAN, a spinster in Dundee, and David Carnie, a bachelor in Dundee, were married in the house of Mrs Bonner, Seagait, Dundee, 16 Jan. 1826. [S]

BONNER, Mrs, a member of the Scots Episcopal Chapel, Castle Street, Dundee, 1824. [DCA.GD.EC.D10.1/3]

BOWEY, CHARLOTTE, dau of Hugh Bowey and Janet Stuart, born 26 Aug, bapt. 6 Sept 1812. [S]

BOYD, DAVID, son of John Boyd and Margaret Pennicuick, born 15 July, bapT. 28 July 1816. [S]

BOYD, JAMES, member of the QEC, 1776. [DCA:GD/EC/D10]

BOYD, MARY, a widow in Dundee, and Thomas Scott, a widower in Dundee, were married in the house of Rev. H. Horseley, Magdalene Yard, Perth Road, Dundee, 30 Oct. 1836. [S]

BOYLE, Mrs, organist, St Paul's, Dundee, 1830. [GD.EC.D10.1-3]

BOYNE, DAVID FARQUHARSON, born 25 Sep., bapt. 4 Oct.1829, 1st son of Alexander Boyne, a ship carpenter, born in Dundee, and his wife Jane, dau. of John Scott, a gardener in Tayfield, Fife. [E]

BRAID, GEORGE, son of William Braid, a flax manufacturer, born in Ceres, Fife, and his wife Agnes, dau. of Patrick Murray, a vintner in Dundee, born 20 Dec 1810, bapt. 14 April 1811. [E]

BRAID, ISABELLA, 8th dau of William Braid, a flax-manufacturer, born in Ceres, Fife, and his wife Agnes, dau of Patrick Murray, a vintner in Dundee, born 15 Aug, bapt. 28 Sept 1809. [E]

BRAID, ROSINA, 9th dau of William Braid, a flax-manufacturer, born in Ceres, Fife, and his wife Agnes, dau of Patrick Murray, a vintner in Dundee, born 17 Mar, bapt. 30 May 1813. [E]

BRAND, ANDREW FIFE, born 6 Dec., bapt. 16 Jan. 1825, 5th son of James Brand, a flax-dresser born in Dundee, and his wife Margaret, dau. of the late Samuel Tinsley, an iron-monger in Colebrookdale, Shropshire, England. [E]

BRAND, ANN, born 4 June, bapt. 17 June 1827, 1st dau. of James Brand, a flax-dresser born in Dundee, and his wife Margaret, dau. of the late Samuel Tinsley, an iron-monger in Colebrookdale, Shropshire, England. [E]

BRAND, JAMES, born 20 Dec., bapt. 30 Dec. 1821, 4th son of James Brand, a flax-dresser born in Dundee, and his wife Margaret, dau. of the late Samuel Tinsley, an iron-monger in Colebrookdale, Shropshire, England. [E]

BRAND, JOHN, member of the QEC, 1776. [DCA:GD/EC/D10]

BRAND, THOMAS, born 3 Feb., bapt. 12 Mar.1820, 3rd son of James Brand, a flax-dresser born in Dundee, and his wife Margaret, dau. of the late Samuel Tinsley an iron-monger in Colebrookdale, Shropshire. England. [E]; a member of the Scots Episcopal Chapel, Castle Street, Dundee, 1824. [DCA.GD.EC.D10.1/3]

BRECHIN, DAVID, church member, 1743. [DCA.GD/EC/DIO/2/1]; a gardener, QEC vestryman, 1769; 1776. [DCA:GD/EC/D10]

BRECHIN, DAVID, a mariner, and Elizabeth Sime, both in Dundee, were married 21 Jan.1820. [E]

BRIDGES, Mrs, member of the QEC, 1776. [DCA:GD/EC/D10]

BRIDGETT, MARY, 1st dau of John Bridgett, a Sergeant of the Woolwich Division of the Royal Marines, born in South Taunton, Devon, England, and his wife Mary Bear, dau of William Bear, born in South Taunton, was born 3 Nov, bapt 20 Nov. 1808. [E]

BROMLEE, ANN, 4th dau of Samuel Bromlee. a labourer and Private of the 79th Regiment of Foot, born in Windsor, Berkshire, and his wife Isobel, dau of Alexander Hackett, a shoemaker in Dundee, born 9 Feb, bapt. 18 Feb. 1810. [E]

BROMLEE, CHARLES, 2nd son of Samuel Bromlee, a labourer, born in Windsor, Berkshire, England, and his wife Isabella, dau. of Alexander Hackett, a shoemaker, born in Dundee, born 25 Oct 1807 bapt. 9 July 1809. [E]

BROOKS, JOHN, 2nd son of William Brooks, a seaman, born in Perth, and his wife Margaret, dau. of John Dalrymple, a merchant in Fraserburgh, Aberdeenshire, born 1 May, bapt. 19 May 1814. [E]

BROTCHIE, JANE ALEXANDER, 1st dau of John Brotchie, a Private of the 79th Regiment of Foot, born in Dunnet, Caithness, and his wife Margaret, dau. of John Gordon, a farmer in Inveraurin, Aberdeenshire, born 27 May bapt. 26 June 1810. [E]

BROWN, ALEXANDER, 2nd son of John Brown, toll-keeper of South Wallace- Craigie, Dundee, born in Linthairn, [Linlathin?, Angus] and his wife Ann, dau of .... Ritchie weaver, born in Dundee, born 16 May, bapt. 21 May 1809. [E]

BROWN, ANN, in Dundee, and William Johnston in Dundee, were married at the house of Rev. John Hetherton, Paton's Lane, Dundee, 25 Oct. 1831. [S]

BROWN, JAMES, son of James Brown and Isabel Mitchell, born 3 Mar., bapt. 17 Mar. 1816. [S]

BROWN, GEORGE, of Horn, Perthshire, 1727. [ECD]

BROWN, GRIZEL, dau of the laird of Horn, Perthshire, bapt. 16 August 1723 [BN]; dead by 1803. [DCA:GD/EC/D10]

BROWN, HELEN, dau of the laird of Horn, Perthshire, bapt. 25 July 1725 [BN]

BROWN, ISABELL, dau of James Brown and Isabell Mitchell, born 17 Mar. bapt. 20 Mar 1815. [S]

BROWN, ISABELLA, 3rd dau of Archibald Brown, a Private of the 79th Regiment of Foot, born in Tiree, Argyll, and   his wife Isabell, dau of Hugh McKay in Kiltern, Ross-shire, born 28 Sept, bapt. 7 Oct 1810. [E]

BROWN, JAMES, church member, 1764, 1784. [DCA.GD/EC/DIO/2/1] [DCA.GD/EC/D10/2/2][E]

BROWN, JOHN, a merchant in Dundee, 1727. [ECD]

BROWN, JOHN, a brewer in Dundee, 1727. [ECD]

BROWN, JOHN, sr, church member, 1743. [DCA.GD/EC/DIO/2/1; 2/3]

BROWN, Captain JOHN, a church member, 1746. [DCA.GD/EC/D10/2/1]

BROWN, Dr JOHN, a church member, 1750. [DCA.GD/EC/DIO/2/1]

BROWN, JOHN, a member QEC, 1776, 1781. [DCA:GD/EC/D10]

BROWN, JOHN HAMILTON, of Glasswell, Angus, a church member, 1784. [DCA.GD/EC/D10/2/2][E]

BROWN, MARGARET, dau of the laird of Horn, Perthshire, bapt. 28 January 1725. [BN]

BROWN, MARY, 2nd dau of James Brown, a gardener, born in Borford, Suffolk, England, and his wife Isabella, dau. of David Kidd, a labourer in Carmyllie, Angus, born 11 Oct. bapt 15 Oct. 1809. [E]

BROWN, ROBERT, in Dundee, 1727. [ECD]; pensioner, 1740. [DCA.GD/EC/DIO/2/1]

BROWN, WILLIAM, a bachelor in Mains parish, Angus, and Anne Rattray, a spinster in Mains parish, Angus, were married 10 Aug. 1823. [S]

BROWN, Miss, sister of John Brown of Glasswell, church member, 1750, 1764. [DCA.GD/EC/DIO/2/1]

BROWNING, ..., a sugar baker, vestryman of the QEC, 1778. [DCA:GD/EC/D10]

BROWNHILL, ANN, born 10 Oct., bapt. 16 Oct. 1825, 2nd dau. of William Brownhill, a weaver, born in Meigle, Perthshire, and his wife Margaret, dau. of the late Jeremy Lynch, a labourer in Little Leagh, County Cork, Ireland. [E]

BRUCE, ANNE, dau of John Bruce and Catherine Phin, born 16 July bapt. 24 Oct 1813. [S]

BRUCE, ANN, born 4 Aug. 1801, bapt. 23 Mar.1825, dau. of James Bruce, a wheelwright in Bonnethill, Dundee, and spouse of Robert Thompson, a square wright and cabinetmaker at West Port of Dundee. [E]

BRUCE, DAVID, 4th son of Robert Bruce a labourer in Couttie's Wynd, Dundee, born in Skene, Aberdeenshire, and his wife Isabella Skene, dau.

of Robert Skene, a labourer in Aberdeen, was born 4 Dec, bapt. 11 Dec 1808. [E]

BRUCE, HELEN, 4th dau. of Robert Bruce, a labourer, born in Skene, Aberdeenshire, and his wife Isabella, dau. of Robert Skene in Skene, born 23 May, bapt. 26 May 1811. [E]

BRUCE, JOHN, a wright, church member, 1777. [DCA:GD/EC/D10/1/2][S]

BRUCE, MARGARET, dau of Patrick Bruce in the Seagait, Dundee, bapt. 27 March 1723. [BN]

BRUCE, WILLIAM, son of Robert Bruce and Janet his wife, born 14 Feb, bapt. 26 Feb 1815. [S]

BRUNTON, GEORGE, a bachelor in St Mary's parish, Edinburgh, married Jane Alexander, a spinster in Dundee, in her father's house in the Murraygait, Dundee, 1 Oct. 1827. [S]

BRYSON, WILLIAM, born 20 Nov.1820, 1st son of William Bryson, a manufacturer in Glasgow born in Glasgow, and his wife Elizabeth, dau. of David Bryson a manufacturer in Glasgow. [E]

BUCHAN, Captain, a vestryman, 1828/1830. [E] [DCA.GD.EC.D10.1/1]

BULLOCH, GEORGE, and Isobell Johnstone, both of Dundee, were married in the house of Rev. John Hetherton, Paton's Lane, Dundee, 13 Dec. 1833. [S]

BULLOCK, GEORGE, born 15 June, bapt. 22 June 1829, 2nd son of Thomas Bullock, a weaver, born in Kileven, County Monaghan, Ireland, and his wife Mary, dau. of William Hannass, a weaver in Kileven, County Monaghan, Ireland. [E]

BUCHAN, DAVID, church member, 1743. [DCA.GD/EC/D10/2/3]

BUCHAN, JAMES, son of David Buchan and Margaret Kidd, born 3 Jan 1815. [S]

BUCHAN,........, vestryman, 1810. [S][DCA:GD/EC/D10.1/2][S]

BUCNEY, JOHN, son of John Bucney and Agnes his wife, born 18 July, bapt. 21 Nov 1813. [S]

BURGESS, JOHN, son of William Burgess and Betty his wife, born 26 Sep. bapt. 13 Oct. 1816. [S]

BURNETT, GEORGE, a wig-maker, vestryman, 1761. [DCA.GD/EC/D10/2/2][E]

BURNET, MARGARET, dau of George Burnet, a wigmaker in Dundee, bapt. 24 March 1725. [BN]

BURNS, JOHN, 1st son of John Burns, a gardener, born in Brechin, Angus, and his wife Mary, born in St Andrews, Fife, dau of William Galloway, a farmer, born 11 Jan, bapt. 18 Jan. 1809. [E]

BURNS, MARIANNE, 4th dau of John Burns, a gardener, born in Brechin, Angus, and his wife Mary, dau of William Galloway farmer, born in St Andrews, Fife, born 14 Aug. bapt. 19 Aug. 1810. [E]

BUSIE, WILLIAM, son of Alexander Busie and Isabel Craigie, bapt. 27 Oct. 1816. [S]

BUTCHART, DAVID, 3rd son of David Butchart, a weaver, born in Forfar Angus, and his wife Sarah, dau. of Daniel Martin, a weaver in Clough, County Antrim, Ireland, born 16 Nov. bapt. 24 Nov. 1811. [E]

BUTCHART, WILLIAM, son of Andrew Butchart, a Private of 2nd Battalion of the .....Regiment, and Christian his wife, born 5 Jan., bapt 17 Jan. 1813. [S]

BUTCHART, Mrs, a member of the Scots Episcopal Chapel, Castle Street, Dundee, 1824. [DCA.GD.EC.D10.1/3]

BUTTER, ROBERT, son of Robert Butter and Elizabeth his wife, born 24 Sept. bapt. 30 Oct. 1814. [S]

BUTTERWORTH, ANNE, dau. of Michael Butterworth and Jessie his wife born 14 Dec. 1814, bapt. 5 Jan. 1815. [S]

BUTTERWORTH, JAMES SMITH, son of Michael Butterworth and his wife Janet, born 11 May, bapt. 9 June 1816. [S]

CABELL, PETER, a weaver in Dundee, a bachelor, married Jean Twiddle a spinster in Dundee, at the house of Mrs Addison, High Street, Dundee, on 21 June 1818. [S]

CADGER, W., 1829. [DCA.GD.EC.D10.1/3]

CAIRNCROSS, JAMES WILSON, son of Thomas Cairncross and .... Scrymgeour, born 12 June, bapt. 23 June 1816. [S]

CAIRNS, ANDREW, 1739. [DCA.GD/EC/DIO/2/1]

CAITHNESS, JOHN, son of David Caithness and Elizabeth his wife, born 8 Dec. bapt. 15 Dec. 1811. [S]

CAITHNESS, Mrs, a member of the Scots Episcopal Chapel, Castle Street, Dundee, 1824. [DCA.GD.EC.D10.1/3]

CAMERON, ALEXANDER, son of John Cameron, a Private of the 1st Battalion of the 79th Regiment of Foot, and Mary his wife, born 2 Feb. bapt. 6 Mar. 1814. [S]

CAMERON, ANN, born 25 Aug., bapt. 18 Oct.1829, 1st dau. of James Cameron, a weaver, born in Ballimony, County Antrim, Ireland, and his wife Janet, dau. of the late William Chisholm a shoemaker in Glamis, Angus. [E]

CAMERON, HELEN, (1), member of the QEC, 1776. [DCA:GD/EC/D10]

CAMERON, HELEN, (2), member of the QEC, 1776. [DCA:GD/EC/D10]

CAMERON, JAMES, church member, 1743. [DCA.GD/EC/DIO/2/1; 2/3]

CAMERON, JOHN, son of James Cameron and Jane his wife, born 9 Nov. bapt. 11 Dec. 1814. [S]

CAMERON, MARGARET, dau of James Cameron and Jane his wife, born 11 May, bapt. 14 June 1812. [S]

CAMERON, MARGARET, dau of James Cameron and Jane his wife, born 21 May, bapt. 5 June 1815. [S]

CAMERON, MARY, born 21 Mar., bapt. 4 Apr. 1820, second dau. of Daniel Cameron, a confectioner born in Edinburgh, and his wife Ann, dau. of the late Charles Butler, a pensioner in Dumfries. [E]

CAMPBELL, ABRAHAM, bachelor in Dundee, married Hannah Roger, a spinster in Dundee, in the vestry of the Scots Episcopal Chapel I Dundee on 21 Oct. 1821. [S]

CAMPBELL, CHRISTI ANNETTE, 1st dau of Daniel Campbell, a mariner, born in Killin, Perthshire, and his wife Anna Sophia, dau of Sir George Putland in Wexford, Ireland, born 24 Dec. 1815, bapt. 6 Jan 1816. [E]

CAMPBELL, DAVID, born 12 May, bapt. 22 May 1829, 1st son of John Campbell, an itinerant book-seller, born in Billy, County Antrim, Ireland, and his wife Janet, dau. of David Pirie an auctioneer in Dundee. [E]

CAMPBELL, ELIZABETH, born 30 July, bapt. 13 Aug. 1826, 1st dau. of John Campbell, a weaver, born in Maghracross, County Fermanagh, Ireland, and his wife Charlotte, dau. of William Elder in Bucklemaker Wynd, Dundee. [E]

CAMPBELL, JOHN, born 21 Nov. bapt. 30 Nov. 1828, 3rd son of William Campbell, a weaver, born in Maghracross, County Fermanagh, Ireland, and his wife Mary, dau. of John Campbell a weaver in Maghracross. [E]

CAMPBELL, MARY, born 12 June, bapt. 22 June 1828, 2nd dau. of John Campbell, a weaver, born in Maghracross, County Fermanagh, Ireland, and his wife Charlotte, dau. of William Elder in Bucklemaker Wynd, Dundee. [E]

CAMPBELL, WILLIAM, born 6 Sep., bapt. 11 Oct. 1825, 3rd son of Richard Campbell, a weaver, born in Drumkearn, County Fermanagh, Ireland, and his wife Edith, dau. of Robert Davis a farmer in Drumkearn, County Fermanagh, Ireland. [E]

CARLISLE, WILLIAM, son of William Carlisle, a Private in the Durham Militia and Jane his wife, born 8 Mar, bapt. 26 June 1814. [E]

CARNEGIE, ANN, born 29 Apr. bapt. 2 May 1824, 1st dau. of David Carnegie, a weaver, born in Monikie, Angus, and his wife Elizabeth dau. of James Bisset, a baker in Muirdrum, Panbride, Angus. [E]

CARNEGIE, Lieutenant JAMES, church member, 1811. [DCA:GD/EC/D10/1/1]

CARNEGIE, JANET, born 6 Jan., bapt. 20 Mar. 1826, 2nd dau. of David Carnegie, a weaver, born in Monikie, Angus, and his wife Elizabeth, dau. of James Bisset, a baker in Muirdrum, Panbride, Angus. [E]

CARNEGY, JOHN, a stabler in Dundee, 1727. [ECD]

CARNEGIE, ROBERT, MD, and Amelia Nimmo, both in Dundee, were married on 1 Oct. 1821. [E]

CARNEGIE, Miss, a vestryman, 1835. [DCA.GD.EC.D10.1-3]

CARNIE, DAVID, a bachelor in Dundee, and Jean Bonner, a spinster in Dundee, were married in the house of Mrs Bonner, in Seagait, Dundee, 16 Jan. 1826. [S]

CARR, ISOBEL, dau. of John Carr, a baker in Murraygait, Dundee, bapt. 24 June 1723. [BN]

CARRIE, MARY, and Samuel Neilson, both in Dundee, were married in the house of Rev. John Hetherton, Paton's Lane, Dundee, 11 Nov. 1834. [S]

CARRUTHERS, DAVID COLVILLE, son of David Carruthers and Margaret his wife, born 30 Mar. 1807, bapt. 2 Nov 1812. [S]

CASWELL, ALEXANDER, 1st son of Thomas Alexander Caswell, a mariner, born in Bridport, Dorset, England, and his wife Mary, dau of Alexander Spalding, a gardener in Dundee, born 8 Nov. bapt. 5 Dec. 1813. [E]

CASWELL, ELISABETH, born 10 Apl., bapt. 18 Apl. 1819, dau. of Thomas Caswell, a mariner born in Bridport, Dorset, England, and his wife Mary, dau. of Alexander Spalding, a gardener in Dundee. [E]

CASWELL, JAMES VINCENT, born 14 Feb., bapt. 16 Mar. 1817, son of Thomas Caswell, a mariner born in Bridport, Dorset, England, and his wife Mary, dau. of Alexander Spalding, a gardener in Dundee. [E]

CASWELL, THOMAS PITCHER, born 8 Nov., bapt. 18 Nov. 1821, 3rd son of Thomas Caswell, a mariner born in Bridport, Dorset, England, and his wife Mary, dau. of Alexander Spalding, a gardener in Dundee. [E]

CASWELL, WILLIAM, born 10 Apl., bapt. 18 Apl. 1819, dau. of Thomas Caswell, a mariner born in Bridport, Dorset, England, and his wife Mary dau. of Alexander Spalding, a gardener in Dundee. [E]

CAW, JAMES, son of Thomas Caw and his wife Anne, born 17 Jan., bapt. 28 Jan. 1816. [S]

CHALMERS, ALEXANDER, born 19 July, bapt. 26 July 1829, 1st son of James Chalmers, a hawker, born in Coupar Angus, Perthshire, and his wife Jane, dau. of the late Alexander Speed in Dundee. [E]

CHALMERS, ANN, born 19 Aug., bapt. 24 Aug. 1828, 2nd dau. of Thomas Chalmers, a weaver, born in Dundee, and his wife Ann, dau. of Thomas Great, a seaman in Dundee. [E]

CHALMERS, BARBARA, dau. of James Chalmers and Barbara his wife, born 26 July, bapt. 10 Aug. 1816. [S]

CHALMERS, CHARLES, and Catharine Hackney, both in Dundee, were married 8 Mar.1819. [E]

CHALMERS, CHARLES, son of James Chalmers and Barbara his wife, born 22 Feb 1815, bapt. 22 Mar 1815. [S]

CHALMERS, ELIZABETH, born 21 Sep., bapt. 8 Oct. 1826, 1st dau. of Thomas Chalmers, a weaver, born in Dundee, and his wife Ann, dau. of Thomas Great, a seaman in Dundee. [E]

CHALMERS, HUGH, a shoemaker, church member, 1777, 1781; 1810. [DCA:GD/EC/D10/1/2][S]

CHALMERS, HUGH, a pensioner aged 80 in 1818. [S][DCA.GD.EC.D10.1/2]

CHALMERS, JAMES, a gardener, church member, 1777. [DCA.GD/EC/D10/1/2][S]

CHALMERS, JAMES, born 1782, a bookseller in Castle Street, Dundee, died 26 Aug. 1853; member of the QEC, 1811. [St Paul's MI] [DCA:GD/EC/D10/1/1]

CHALMERS, JAMES, a vestryman, 1816/1817/1818/1819/1820/1825 /1828/1833. [S][DCA.EC.GD.EC.D10.1/2/3]

CHALMERS, JOHN MILLER, 5th son of James Chalmers, a weaver, born in Glamis, Angus, and his wife Margaret, dau of Alexander Donaldson, a weaver in Kirriemuir, Angus, born 18 Dec. bapt 30 Dec. 1810. [E]

CHALMERS, PHILIP, a shoemaker, church member, 1764, 1777, 1781; 1810. [DCA.GD/EC/D10/1/2][S] [DCA.GD/EC/DIO/2/1]

CHALMERS, ROBERT, son of James Chalmers and Barbara his wife, born 31 Jan. bapt. 11 Mar. 1813. [S]

CHALMERS, Mrs, a member of the Scots Episcopal Chapel, Castle Street, Dundee, 1824; among the 'poor of St Paul's 1830' [DCA.GD.EC.D10.1/3]

CHRYSTAL, GEORGE, born 13 Sep., bapt. 4 Oct. 1828, 4th son of William Christal, a sailor, born in Dundee, and his wife Margaret, dau. of James Goodlet, a weaver in Dundee. [E]

CHRISTAL, JAMES, born 5 Dec. bapt. 15 Dec. 1822, 1st son of William Christal, a sailor, born in Dundee, and his wife Margaret, dau. of James Goodlet, a weaver in Dundee. [E]

CHRISTAL, JOHN, born 6 Oct. bapt. 12 Nov. 1826, 3rd son of William Christal, a sailor, born in Dundee, and his wife Margaret, dau. of James Goodlet, a weaver in Dundee. [E]

CHRISTAL, WILLIAM, born 28 Aug. bapt. 19 Sep. 1824, 2nd son of William Christal, a sailor, born in Dundee, and his wife Margaret, dau. of James Goodlet, a weaver in Dundee. [E]

CHRISTIE, ALEXANDER, a writer, [lawyer], member of the Scots Episcopal Chapel, Castle Street, Dundee, 1824; vestryman, 1833 [DCA.GD.EC.D10.1/3]

CHRISTIE, CATHERINE, dau of Alexander Christie and Catherine his wife, born 12 June, bapt. 3 July 1815. [S]

CHRISTIE, FRANCES GROVES, born 20 Mar., bapt. 13 Apr. 1823, 2nd dau. of John Christie, a travelling merchant, born in Belfast, Ireland, and his wife Ann, dau. of Neil MacFey a labourer in Glasgow. [E]

CHRISTIE, ISABELLA, born 6 Oct. bapt. 12 Nov. 1820, 4th dau. of Alexander Christie, a writer [lawyer] born in Arbuthnott, Kincardineshire, and his wife Catherine, dau. of Andrew Binny, stamp-master in Forfar, Angus. [E]

CHRISTIE, JOHN, born 29 Mar., bapt. 30 Apr. 1828, 1st son of John Christie, a travelling merchant, born in Belfast, Ireland, and his wife Ann, dau. of Neil MacFey, a labourer in Glasgow. [E]

CHRISTIE, MATILDA, dau. of James Christie and Margaret Thow, born 8 July, bapt. 11 Aug. 1816. [S]

CHRISTIE, ..., member of the QEC, 1776. [DCA:GD/EC/D10/1/1]

CLARK, AGNES, dau. of Thomas Clark and his wife Jane, born 4 Dec., bapt. 28 Dec. 1816. [S]

CLARK, ANDREW, born 18 Aug., bapt. 24 Aug. 1832, son of George Clark, a white smith from Kilmartin, Argyll and his wife Isabella. [E]

CLARK, BETSY THOM, dau. of Francis Clark and Agnes Bertie, born 5 Mar. bapt. 30 Aug 1812. [S]

CLARK, CATHERINE, 2nd dau. of Robert Clark, a Sergeant of the 25th Regiment of Foot, born in Aughbone, County Monaghan, Ireland, and his wife Ann, dau of William Wilkie, a shoemaker, born in Aughbone, born 27 May, bapt 11 June 1809. [E]

CLARK, CHARLES, a vestryman, St Paul's, 1831/1833. [DCA.GD.EC.D10.1-3]

CLARK, ISABEL, dau. of Thomas Clark and Jane his wife, born 29 Jan, bapt. 12 Feb 1815. [S]

CLARK, JAMES, son of Saunders Clark and Nancy his wife, born 9 June, bapt. 16 June 1813. [S]

CLARK, JANE, dau. of Saunders Clark and Agnes his wife, born 14 Feb. bapt. 18 Feb. 1816. [S]

CLARK, JOHN, born 9 Nov. bapt. 17 Nov.1835, son of Richard Clark a tinman. [E]

CLARK, MARTHA, bapt. 20 Jan. 1834, infant dau. of George Clark and his wife Isabella. [E]

CLARK, MARY, dau. of Thomas Clark and Jane his wife, born 27 Apr, bapt. 19 May 1812. [S]

CLARK, ..., organist of the QEC, 1789. [DCA:GD/EC/D10/1/1] [DCA.GD/EC/D10/2/2][E]

CLARK, ..., 1829. [DCA.GD.EC.D10.1/3]

CLAYHILLS, ALEXANDER, of Invergowrie, Perthshire, a bachelor in Dundee, and Elizabeth Hunter, in spinster of Rescobie, Angus, were married in the house of Lieutenant General Hunter in Broughty Ferry Angus, 10 Oct. 1826. [S]; a member of the Scots Episcopal Chapel, Castle Street, Dundee, 1824; vestryman, 1830. [DCA.GD.EC.D10.1/3]

CLAYHILLS, JAMES, of Invergowrie, Perthshire, vestryman of the QEC, 1807, 1810. [DCA:GD/EC/D10/1/1]

CLAYHILLS, JAMES, a vestryman, 1817/1825; a member of the Scots Episcopal Chapel, Castle Street, Dundee, 1824. [S]

CLEMENT, HELKERTON, 2nd son of James Clement, a weaver, born in Dundee, and his wife Jane, dau of David Miller, a shoemaker in Dundee born 24 Sept., bapt. 27 Sept. 1812. [E]

CLEMENT, JOHN ROSS, born 18 June, bapt. 5 July 1818, son of James Clement, a weaver, born in Dundee, and his wife Jane Miller, dau. of David Miller, a shoemaker in Dundee. [E]

CLEMENT, MONTGOMERY, born 26 June, bapt. 7 July 1816, son of James Clement, a weaver, born in Dundee, and his wife Jane Miller, dau. of David Miller, a shoemaker in Dundee. [E]

CLEMENT, WALTER SHAW, born 5 Dec., bapt. 16 Dec. 1827, 2nd son of James Clement, overseer at a spinning mill, and his wife Catharine, dau. of John Shaw a farmer. [E]

CLERK, JAMES, son of James Clerk and Mary Gray, born 8 Dec. 1816, bapt. 19 Jan. 1817. [S]

CLIPPERT, Mrs, member of the QEC, 1776. [DCA:GD/EC/D10/1/1]

COBB, DAVID, a writer [lawyer] in Dundee, 1825/1828. [DCA.GD.EC.D10.1/3]

COCK, ROBERT, 1784. [DCA.GD/EC/D10/2/2][E]

COLBERT, HENRY, born 11 July, bap. 16 Sep. 1818, son of George Colbert, a printer born in Dundee, and his wife Susannah Daley, dau. of Thomas Swinburne in London. [E]

COLLIN, ELIZABETH, born 14 Jan., bap.2 May 1827, 3rd dau. of Thomas Collin, a weaver, born in Maghracross, County Fermanagh, Ireland, and his wife Elizabeth, dau. of the late William Robinson a tailor in Maghracross, County Fermanagh. [E]

COLLIN, JANE, born 2 June, bap.2 Aug. 1828, 4th dau. of Thomas Collin, a weaver, born in Maghracross, County Fermanagh, Ireland, and his wife Elizabeth, dau. of the late William Robinson a tailor in Maghracross, Co. Fermanagh. [E]

COLMAN, ISABELLA, born 39 May, bap. 7 June 1829, 1st dau. of James Colman, a basket maker, born in Dublin, Ireland, and his wife Isabella, dau. of Andrew Ross a hatter in Dundee. [E]

COLMAN, JAMES, and Isabel Ross, both in Dundee, were married in Broughty Ferry, Angus, on 14 Sep.1826. [E]

COLQUHOUN, Mrs, relict of William Colquhoun or Calhoun, pensioner, 1739. [DCA.GD/EC/DIO/2/1]

COLVILL, Mr, member of the QEC, 1776. [DCA:GD/EC/D10/1/1]

CONNOR, EDWARD MIDDLETON, son of James Connor and Agnes his wife, born 10 Mar, bapt 12 Apr 1812. [S]

CONSTABLE, DAVID, a flesher, [butcher], church member, 1743, 1746. [DCA.GD/EC/DIO/2/1; 2/3]

CONSTABLE, GEORGE, church member, 1784. [DCA.GD/EC/D10/2/2][E]

CONSTABLE, JOHN, a butcher in Dundee, 1727. [ECD]

COOKE, ANDREW SMITH BARNES, born 13 Mar., bapt. 3 Apl. 1826, 3rd son of William Cooke, a liquor and spirit merchant born in Irvine, Ayrshire, and his wife Jane, dau. of late Francis Connel a weaver in Glasgow. [E]

COOKE, CATHARINE, born 16 Nov. bapt. 26 Nov.1829, third dau. of William Cooke, a stoneware merchant, born in Irvine, and his wife Jane, dau. of late Francis Connel a weaver in Glasgow. [E]

COOK, DAVID, son of James Cook, a dyer in Murraygait, Dundee, bapt. 4 March 1725. [BN]

COOK, ELIZABETH, dau of James Cook and Isabell his wife, born 14 July, bapt. 26 July 1812. [S]

COOKE, GEORGE, born 15 Aug., bapt. 27 Aug.1822, 1st son of William Cooke, a stoneware merchant, born in Irvine, Ayrshire, and his wife Jane, dau. of late Francis Connel, a weaver in Glasgow. [E]

COOK, ISABEL, dau. of James Cook and Isabel his wife, born 20 May, bapt. 3 June 1816. [S]

COOKE, JAMES, born 19 June, bapt. 28 July 1824, 2nd son of William Cooke, a stoneware merchant, born in Irvine, Ayrshire, and his wife Jane, dau. of late Francis Connel, a weaver in Glasgow. [E]

COOK, JOHN, church member, 1743. [DCA.GD/EC/DIO/2/1; 2/3]

COOK, JOHN, a dyer, church member, 1764, 1777, 1781. [DCA:GD/EC/D10/1/2][S][DCA.GD/EC/DIO/2/1]

COOK, MARGARET, dau. of James Cook and Isabell his wife, born 4 May, bapt. 31 May 1814. [S]

COOK, MARY ANN, dau. of Robert Cook and Elizabeth his wife, born 29 Dec. 1811 bapt. 19 Jan 1812. [S]

COOKE, WILLIAM LINN, born 25 Oct., bapt. 16 Nov. 1828, 4th son of William Cooke, a stoneware merchant born in Irvine, Ayrshire, and his wife Jane, dau. of late Francis Connel, a weaver in Glasgow. [E]

COOK, Miss, member of the QEC, 1776. [DCA:GD/EC/D10/1/1]

COOPER, JAMES, member of the QEC, 1776. [DCA:GD/EC/D10/1/1]

COPELAND, WILLIAM, son of Henry Copeland, a Private of the 25th Regiment of Foot, born in Binley, Warwickshire, England, and his wife Margaret Tate, dau. of John Tate, bricklayer, born in Alnwick, Northumberland, England, born 24 Jan, bapt. 20 Mar 1809. [E]

CORSAR, ANN, dau. of Frederick Corsar, a merchant in Dundee, bapt. 18 July 1726, the laird of Invergowrie in Perthshire, was godfather while his wife and dau. Mrs Ann Clayhills were godmothers. [BN]

CORSAR, ELIZABETH, dau. of Frederick Corsar, a merchant in Dundee, bapt. 12 Mar 1725, the laird of Invergowrie in Perthshire was godfather while lady Invergowrie and their dau. Mrs Margaret Clayhills were godmothers. [BN]

COSTLEY, AGNES, born 5 Oct., bapt. 1 Nov. 1828, 2nd dau. of George Costley, a weaver, born in Danyclones, County Down, Ireland, and his wife Elizabeth, dau. of Archibald MacChesnut, a weaver in Ballintoy, County Antrim, Ireland. [E]

COSTLEY, SARAH, born 10 Sep., bapt. 28 Oct. 1827, 2nd dau. of John Costley, a weaver, born in Marlin, County Down, Ireland, and his wife Jane, dau. of William Benwicks, steward to Mr Douglas of Gracefield, County Down. [E]

COUPAR, HENRY, son of James Coupar in Cotterton of Craigie, Dundee, bapt. 28 Feb 1725. [BN]

COUPAR, JAMES, 1727. [ECD]

COUPAR, JOHN, and Anne Couper, both in Dundee, were married 19 Mar 1809. [E]

COUPAR, PATRICK, 1727. [ECD]

COUPAR, THOMAS, shipmaster in Dundee, a bachelor, married Helen Hackney, a spinster in Aberlemno, Angus, at the house of David Caithness, a shipmaster in Dundee, 20 Dec. 1817. [S]

COURTNEY, ..., vestryman, 1814. [S][DCA: GD/EC/D10.1/2][S]

COUTY, JANE, born 17 Mar., bapt. 28 Mar. 1819, 1st dau. of William Couty, a weaver, born in Forfar, Angus, and his wife Margaret, dau. of John Jack, a hostler in Forfar. [E]

COWELL, WILLIAM HENRY, born 30 Dec.1822, bapt. 12 Jan.1823, 1st son of William Cowell, Sergeant of the 67th Regiment of Foot, born in

Worcester, England, and his wife Marianne, dau. of Henry Pinche {?}, in Bishop Walton, Hampshire, England. [E]

COWEN, ELIZA, 2nd dau. of Thomas Cowen, Lieutenant of the 79th Regiment of Foot, born in Newry, County Down, Ireland, and his wife Mary, dau of Robert Hopper, a merchant in Mullingal, County Meath, Ireland, born 9 Aug, bapt 1 Sept 1815. [E]

COWIE, JAMES, a tinsmith, and Helen Gowans, both in Dundee, were married 2 Feb.1823. [E]

COWIE, JAMES, born 24 Feb., bap. 14 Mar. 1824, 1st son of James Cowie a tinsmith, born in Dundee, and his wife Helen, dau. of the late Robert Gowans, a flax dresser in Dundee. [E]

COWIE, JOHN, born 13 Feb., bap. 4 Mar. 1827, 2nd son of James Cowie, a tinsmith, born in Dundee, and his wife Helen, dau. of the late Robert Gowans, a flax dresser in Dundee. [E]

COWIE, MARGARET, dau. of David Cowie, a Private in the 25th Regiment of Foot, born 22 Apr. bapt. 2 May 1813. [S]

COX, ..., member of the QES, 1776. [DCA:GD/EC/D10/1/1]

CRABB, ALEXANDER, 2nd son of John Crabb, a mariner, born in Dundee, and his wife Janet, dau of James Chalmers a weaver in Dundee, born 12 June, bapt. 21 June 1813. [E]

CRABB, ESTHER, born 11 Apr., bapt. 21 Apr. 1825, 4th son of John Crabb a mariner, born in Dundee, and his wife Janet, dau. of James Chalmers, a weaver in Dundee. [E]

CRABB, HELEN MILLER, 1st dau of John Crabb, a mariner, born in Dundee, and his wife Janet, dau. of James Chalmers weaver in Dundee, born 1 Aug. bapt. 6 Aug. 1815. [E]

CRABB, JAMES, 1st son of John Crabb, a mariner, born in Dundee, and his wife Janet, dau of James Chalmers weaver in Dundee, born 9 Mar. bapt. 21 Mar. 1813. [E]

CRABB, JANE, born 16 Sept. bapt. 17 Sept. 1820, 2nd dau. of John Crabb, a mariner, born in Dundee, and his wife Janet, dau. of James Chalmers, a weaver in Dundee. [E]

CRABB, JOHN, a sailor, and Janet Chalmers, both in Dundee, were married 2 Feb. 1812. [E]

CRABBE, JOHN, son of David Crabbe and Euphemia Nicoll, born 14 July, bapt. 19 Sept. 1813. [S]

CRAIG, ANN, born 28 May, bapt. 11 June 1820, 3rd dau. of Robert Craig, a travelling chapman, born in Kilmonachan, County West Meath, Ireland, and his wife Mary, daughter of Andrew Reid, a founder, late of Dundee. [E]

CRAIG, MARY ANN, born 4 Sept. bapt. 12 Sept. 1824, 4th dau. of Robert Craig, late a travelling chapman now a carter, born in Kilmonachan, County West Meath, Ireland, and his wife Mary, daughter of Andrew Reid, a founder, late of Dundee. [E]

CRAIG, MATTHEW, born 11 Jan. bapt. 28 Jan. 1827, 7th son of Robert Craig, late a travelling chapman now a carter, born in Kilmonachan, County West Meath, Ireland, and his wife Mary, daughter of Andrew Reid, a founder, late of Dundee. [E]

CRAIG, ROBERT, born 4 Oct. bapt. 13 Oct. 1822, 8th son of Robert Craig a travelling chapman born in Kilmonachan, County West Meath, Ireland, and his wife Mary, daughter of Andrew Reid, a founder late of Dundee. [E]

CRAIGHEAD, JAMES, son of James Craighead in Mains parish, Angus, bapt. 15 Oct. 1725. [BN] [ECD]

CRAMOND, ALEXANDER, born 22 Dec. 1817, bapt. 13 Feb. 1818, son of John Cramond, a weaver, born in Dundee, and his wife Strachan (sic), dau. of James Peacock in Forfar, Angus. [E]

CRAMOND, WALTER PEACOCK, born 7 July, bapt. 23 July 1820, second son of John Cramond, a weaver, born in Dundee, and his wife Strachan (sic), dau. of James Peacock in Forfar, Angus. [E]

CRAWFORD, DAVID, son of the laird of Monorgan, Perthshire, bapt. 19 Aug. 1724, James Paton minister at Catness [Kettins?, Angus] and Thomas Crichton, a surgeon apothecary were godfathers while Mr Paton's wife was godmother. [BN]

CRAWFORD, JAMES, son of the laird of Monorgan, Perthshire, bapt. 12 July 1723, James Paton, minister in Catness [Kettins, Angus], and Thomas Crichton, an apothecary in Dundee, were godfather and Mr Paton's wife was godmother. [BN]

CRAWFORD, JAMES, a merchant in Dundee, QEC committee, 1757; vestryman 1768; 1776; 1784. [DCA:GD/EC/D10/1/1] [DCA.GD/EC/D10/2/2][E]

CRAWFORD, JOHN, son of the laird of Monorgan, Perthshire, bapt. 3 Feb. 1725, Dr John Blair and the laird of Milnhill were godfathers and the lady of Thomas Crichton, a surgeon apothecary in Dundee, was godmother. [BN]

CREIGHTON, ALEXANDER, 1727. [ECD]

CREIGHTON, ALEXANDER, son of Andrew Creighton and Janet Meldrum, born 25 Oct 1811, bapt. 5 Feb 1812. [S]

CRICHTON, ALEXANDER and ELIZABETH, twin children of Patrick Crichton in Seagait, Dundee bapt. 8 Oct. 1726, James Fotheringham, a merchant, and James Johnston, a writer [lawyer], both in Dundee, were godfathers, while the godmothers were the wives of David Fotheringham and Robert Man, merchants in Dundee. [BN] [ECD]

CRICHTON, ANNA, dau. of Thomas Crichton, surgeon apothecary in Dundee, bapt. 5 May 1725, the laird of Monorgan in Perthshire, was godfather while the mother of Mrs Thomas Crichton and Mrs Ogilvy relict of Ogilvy of Newhall in Angus, the younger were godmothers. [BN]

CRICHTON, CLEMENTINA ANN MARGARET, dau. of Thomas Crichton, a surgeon apothecary in Dundee, was bapt. 28 Nov. 1723, the laird of Monorgan in Perthshire, was godfather while Mr Crichton's mother and the lady of Dr Fotheringham were godmothers. [BN]

CRICHTON, DAVID, son of Alexander Crichton in the Seagait, Dundee, was bapt. 9 April 1723. [BN] [a Jacobite in 1745]

CRICHTON, ELIZABETH, dau of Thomas Crichton, a surgeon apothecary in Dundee, was bapt. 3 February 1724, the laird of Monorgan in Perthshire was godfather while Lady Kinloch and Mr Crichton's mother were godmothers. [BN]

CRICHTON, HENRY, son of Thomas Crichton, a surgeon apothecary in Dundee, was bapt. 7 Dec. 1722, James Kinloch of that Ilk and Henry Crawford laird of Monorgan in Perthshire, were godfathers, and lady .... Thomas Crichton's sister was godmother. [BN]

CRICHTON, PATRICK, son of Patrick Crichton of Crunan, was bapt. 20 Nov. 1725, Dr David Fotheringham and Dr Kinloch were godfathers and Mistress Landels was godmother. [BN]

CRICHTON, PATRICK, a tailor, church member, 1777. [DCA:GD/EC/D10/1/2][S]

CRICHTON, THOMAS, of Millhill, Angus, church member, 1777, 1781. [DCA:GD/EC/D10/1/2][S]

CROCKAT, JOHN, a merchant in Dundee, 1727. [ECD]

CROCKAT, Miss, a church member, 1746. [DCA.GD/EC/D10/2/1]

CROLL, CATHERINE, born 5 Sep. bapt. 24 Sep. 1826, 2nd dau. of Alexander Croll, a starch maker, born in Montrose, Angus, and his wife Catherine, dau. of Alexander Gregg a mariner in Dundee. [E]

CROLL, GEORGE OGILVY, born 28 Mar. 1828, bapt. 15 Feb.1829, son of Margaret, dau. of the late James Brown, a wright in Dundee. [E]

CROLL, JOHN, born 1 Jan., bapt. 1 Feb. 1829, 1st son of Alexander Croll, a labourer, born in Montrose, Angus, and his wife Catherine, dau. of Alexander Gregg, a mariner in Dundee. [E]

CROMBIE, ALEXANDER, a wright, church member, 1777. [DCA:GD/EC/D10/1/2][S]

CROOKS, MARGARET, a spinster in Dundee, and James Gillespie, a bachelor in Dundee, were married in the house of Rev. H. Horsley Magdalene Yard, Perth Road, Dundee, 22 Jan. 1836. [S]

CROSBY, JOHN, son of John Crosby and Christian his wife, born 16 Oct. bapt. 24 Oct. 1813. [S]

CRYSTAL, JOHN, 1784. [DCA.GD/EC/D10/2/2][E]

CULBERT, ROBERT, church officer, 1740. [DCA.GD/EC/DIO/2/1]

CUNNINGHAME, ALEXANDER, son of Alexander Cunningham, a Private of the 79th Regiment of Foot, and his wife Mary, bapt. 28 July 1811. [S]

CUTHBERT, JAMES, pensioner, 1739. [DCA.GD/EC/DIO/2/1]

CUTHBERT, JESS, a spinster in Dundee, and James Stirling, a widower in Forfar, Angus, were married in the vestry of St Paul's, Castle Street, Dundee, on 15 Oct. 1826. [S]

DAHNNS, CHRISTIAN GEORGE DANIEL, a sugar baker, [possibly from the Netherlands], and Margaret Kinnear, both in Dundee, were married 24 Dec. 1809. [E]

DAKERS, THOMAS, born 14 Dec.1827, bapt. 27 Jan. 1828, 1st son of Peter Dakers, a flax dresser, born in Brechin, Angus, and his wife Margaret, dau. of John Wood, a flax dresser in Brechin. [E]

DALL, JOHN, pensioner, 1739. [DCA.GD/EC/DIO/2/1]

DALY, ELIZABETH, a widow in Dundee, married James Williamson, a bachelor in Dundee, at the house of Lieutenant General C. Mackenzie in Broughty Ferry, Angus, 31 Oct. 1821. [S]

DAVIDSON, AGNES, 1st dau of Archibald Davidson, a shoemaker, born in Girvan, Ayrshire, and his wife Susannah, dau. of Samuel Siles in Thorn, Yorkshire, England, born 28 June, bapt. 1 July 1810. [E]

DAVIDSON, ALEXANDER, 3rd son of Andrew Davidson weaver, born in Dundee, and his wife Jane, dau. of Francis Arbuthnott, a carrier, born in Benholm, Kincardineshire, born 3 Aug. bapt. 10 Sept. 1809. [E]

DAVIDSON, ELIZABETH, 1st dau of James Davidson, a Private of the 72nd Regiment of Foot, born in Dundee, and his wife Ann, dau. of James, Greg, a spoon-maker, born in Rathen, Aberdeenshire, born 17 Aug. bapt. 10 Sep. 1809. [E]

DAVIDSON, ELIZABETH, 2nd dau of Alexander Davidson, a weaver, born in Dundee, and his wife Jane, dau of Francis Arbuthnot carrier in Benholm, Kincardineshire, born 13 Feb. bapt. 9 Apr. 1812. [E]

DAVIDSON, Mrs JAMES, church member, 1750. [DCA.GD/EC/DIO/2/1]

DAVIDSON, JANE, 2nd dau. of Archibald Davidson shoemaker, born in Girvan, Ayrshire, and his wife Susannah, dau. of Samuel Siles in Thorn, Yorkshire, England born 13 Apr. bapt. 18 Apr. 1813. [E]

DAVIDSON, MATHEW, pensioner, 1743. [DCA.GD/EC/D10/2/1]

DAVIDSON, THOMAS, a writer, [lawyer], clerk-depute, vestryman of the QEC, 1778, 1784. [DCA:GD/EC/D10/1/1] [DCA.GD/EC/D10/2/2]

DAVIDSON, THOMAS, vestryman of the English Chapel, 1808/ 1809/ 1823/1828/1830. [E] [DCA.GD.EC.D10.1/1/3]

DAVIDSON, Mr, member of the QEC, 1776. [DCA:GD/EC/D10/1/1]

DAVIDSON, Miss, member of the QEC, 1776. [DCA:GD/EC/D10/1/1]

DAVIES, RACHEL, dau. of Thomas Davies and Margery Butchard his wife, born 5 Oct. bapt. 6 Dec. 1812. [S]

DAWSON, MARGARET, 7th dau. of William Dawson shoemaker, born in Inverness, and his wife Catherine, dau. of William Patience, a mariner in Inverness, born 10 Apr. bapt. 20 Apr. 1815. [E]

DAWSON, NELLY, dau. of Robert Dawson and Katherine Small, born 7 Oct. bapt. 19 Nov 1815. [S]

DEMPSTER, GEORGE, born 1678, son of Reverend John Dempster, a merchant in Dundee 1727, later of Dunnichen, Angus, a church member 1743, 1746, died 2 June 1753, husband of Margaret Rait. [ECD] [F.5.362/365] [DCA.GD/EC/DIO/2/1; 2/3]

DEMPSTER, GEORGE, of Dunnichen, Angus, 1784. [DCA.GD/EC/D10/2/2][E]

DEMPSTER, JAMES, born 1 Jan. bapt. 7 Jan. 1816, son of Thomas Dempster, Sergeant of the 79th Regiment, born in Dornoch, Sutherland, and his wife Margaret Brisbane, dau. of James Brisbane, a mariner in Greenock, Renfrewshire.[E]

DEMPSTER, JOHN, of Dunnichen, Angus, church member, 1750. [DCA.GD/EC/DIO/2/1]

DEMPSTER Mrs, member QEC, 1776. [DCA:GD/EC/D10/1/1]

DEWAR, JAMES, son of Robert Dewar and Catherine his wife, born 6 Dec. 1813, bapt. 16 Jan. 1814. [S]

DICK, WILLIAM, merchant, QEC vestryman, 1768; member 1776. [DCA:GD/EC/D10/1/1] [DCA.GD/EC/D10/2/2][E]

DICKINSON, JAMES, born 12 June, bapt. 24 June 1821, 2nd son of Robert Dickinson, a blacksmith in Bedlington, County Durham, England, and his wife Mary, dau. of Robert Brown, a blacksmith in Swelwell, Whickham, County Durham. [E]

DICKINSON, MARJORY, born 1 July, bapt. 18 July 1819, 5th dau. of Robert Dickinson, a blacksmith in Bedlington, County Durham, England,

and his wife Mary, dau. of Robert Brown a blacksmith in Swelwell, Whickham, County Durham. [E]

DICKIE, JOHN, member of the QEC, 1776. [DCA:GD/EC/D10/1/1]

DICKSON, DAVID, and Elizabeth Munroe, both in Dundee, were married 7 Jan. 1826. [E]

DIXON, GEORGE, born 4 July. bapt. 11 July 1819, first son of George Dixon a labourer born in Storbridge, Staffordshire, England, and his wife Margaret, dau. of John Mackay, a labourer in Tongue, Ross-shire. [E]

DIVINE, ROBERT, 2nd son of Richard Divine, a drummer in the 79th Regiment of Foot, born in Dublin, Ireland, and his wife Margaret, dau. of the late James Gilchrist, a mariner in Dundee, born 30 Oct. bapt. 5 Nov. 1815. [E]

DOCTOR, ANDREW, pensioner, 1740. [DCA.GD/EC/DIO/2/1]

DOIG, ALEXANDER, pensioner, 1740. [DCA.GD/EC/DIO/2/1]

DOIG, JANET, pensioner, 1746. [DCA.GD/EC/D10/2/1]

DOLLARD, ANN, a spinster in Dundee, and Andrew Scolin, a bachelor in Dundee, were married in the vestry of St Paul's, Castle Street, Dundee, 18 Feb. 1831. [S]

DON, ALEXANDER, church member, 1764. [DCA.GD/EC/DIO/2/1]

DON, JOHN, son of Mathew Don and Janet Ballantyne, born 21 July. bapt. 5 May 1816. [S]

DONALDSON, BETTY, among the 'poor of Mr Hetherton's congregation, 1830' [DCA.GD.EC.D10.1/3]

DONALDSON, ISABELLA, born 25 Nov. bapt. 10 Dec. 1820, first dau. of Alexander Donaldson, a labourer born in Halkrig, Caithness, and his wife Ann, dau. of Robert Bruce, a labourer in Dundee. [E]

DONALDSON, JAMES, son of Andrew Donaldson and Isabella Henderson, born 12 Aug. 1813, bapt. 20 Feb. 1814. [S]

DONALDSON, JEAN, dau. of William Donaldson, a merchant in Dundee, was bapt. 26 May 1723. [BN]

DONALDSON, MARGARET SINCLAIR, born 2 Oct., bap. 13 Nov. 1825, 2nd dau. of Alexander Donaldson, a labourer, born in Halkirk, Caithness, and his wife Ann, dau. of the late Robert Bruce a labourer in Dundee. [E]

DONALDSON, WILLIAM, a merchant in Dundee, 1727. [ECD]

DONALDSON, ROBERT, born 9 Oct., bap. 13 Oct. 1822, 1st son of Alexander Donaldson, a labourer, born in Halkirk, Caithness, and his wife An, dau. of Robert Bruce a labourer in Dundee. [E]

DORIT, JAMES, pensioner, 1740. [DCA.GD/EC/DIO/2/1]

DOUGLAS, Dr ALEXANDER, a vestryman QEC, 1764, 1768; 1776. [DCA:GD/EC/D10/1/1]

DOUGLAS, Sir ALEXANDER, a church member in 1784. [DCA.GD/EC/D10/2/2][E]

DOUGLAS, Sir ALEXANDER, of Glenbervie, Kincardineshire, a vestryman, QEC, 1802, 1810. [DCA.GD/EC/D10/1/2][S]

DOUGLAS, SUSAN NEIL, born 18 Nov., bap. 10 Dec.1826, 1st dau. of James Douglas, a blacksmith, born in Dundee, and his wife Jane, dau. of Andrew Brown, a shoemaker in Dundee. [E]

DOUGLAS, WILLIAM, of Bridgeton, vestryman of the QEC, 1768; 1776, 1784. [DCA:GD/EC/D10/1/1] [DCA.GD/EC/D10/2/2][E]

DOUGLAS, WILLIAM RIDDOCH, 1st son of Thomas Douglas, a gardener, born in Dundee, and his wife Margaret, dau of Thomas Kay, a gardener in Coatbridge, Lanarkshire, born 10 Dec, bapt 24 Dec 1809. [E]

DOUGLAS, WILLIAM GIBB, born 13 Jan., bap. 13 Feb.1825, 4th son of James Douglas, a blacksmith, born in Dundee, and his wife Jane, dau. of Andrew Brown, a shoemaker in Dundee. [E]

DOUGLAS, Captain, a member of the Scots Episcopal Chapel, Castle Street, Dundee,1824. [DCA.GD.EC.D10.1/3]

DOUN, JAMES, son of James Doun and Margaret his wife, born 15 Apr, bapt 31 May 1814. [S]

DOW, ELEANOR, wife of John Anderson, a weaver in Chapelshade, Dundee, born 1739, died 15 December 1808. [E]

DRUMMOND, JAMES, son of George Drummond and Janet his wife, born 15 June, bap. 23 June 1816. [S]

DRUMMOND, THOMAS, a clerk, a church member in 1810.
[DCA.GD/EC/D10/1/2][S]

DRYSDALE, GEORGE, son of George Drysdale and Isabel his wife, born 16 Apl., bap. 28 Apl. 1816. [S]

DUCAT, JAMES STEWART, a Writer to the Signet, parish of St Stephen, Edinburgh, and Catherine Steele, spinster in the parish of St Cuthbert, Edinburgh, were married in the house of Mrs George Greig, Tay Square, Dundee, 9 Sep. 1834. [S]

DUCAT, WILLIAM, a bachelor in Kinnettles, Angus, married Mary Gray, a spinster in Dundee, at the house of Mrs Gray, Tay Square, Dundee, on 29 Mar. 1819. [S]

DUFF, ALEXANDER SMALL, son of John Duff and his wife Janet, born 29 Dec. 1816, bap. 12 Jan. 1817. [S]

DUFF, HELENAS WHYTE, son of John Duff and Jane his wife, born 18 July, bapt 31 July 1814. [S]

DUFF, HENRY, son of John Duff and Jane his wife, born 24 Oct, bapt 7 Nov 1812. [S]

DUFF, JAMES, surveyor, vestryman QEC, 1769; 1776
[DCA:GD/EC/D10/1/1]

DUFF, JAMES, vestryman of the English Chapel, 1808. [E]

DUFF, JOHN, merchant, vestryman of the English Chapel, 1777, 1808. [E] [DCA:GD/EC/D10/1/1] [DCA.GD/EC/D10/2/2][E]

DUFF, JOHN, a surveyor, church member, 1784. [DCA.GD/EC/D10/2/2][E]

DUFF, JOHN, wright, church member, 1810. [DCA.GD/EC/D10/1/2][S]

DUFF, JOHN, clerk, 1816/1817/1818. [S][DARC.GD.EC.D10.1/2]

DUFF, JOHN, vestryman, 1823. [E] [GD.EC.D10.1/1]

DUFF, MARIANNE, born 11 July, bap. 20 July 1828, 1st dau. of Robert Duff, a millwright, born in Leslie, Fife, and his wife Catherine, dau. of Peter Robinson a sailor in Lochee, Dundee. [E]

DUFF, Captain later Major ROBERT, vestryman of the QEC, 1791, 1797, 1804. [DCA:GD/EC/D10/1/1] [DCA.GD/EC/D10/2/2][E]

DUMAN, ANN, 3rd dau of Jacob Duman, a sugar refiner, born in Hanover, Germany, and his wife Mary, dau of Henry Bristow Hartshorn, a manufacturer in Ayliff Street, Whitechapel, London, born 6 Aug, bapt 25 Aug 1811. [E]

DUMAN, CATHARINE, 4th dau of Jacob Duman, a sugar refiner, born in Hanover, Germany, and his wife Mary, dau of Henry Bristow Hartshorn, a manufacturer in Ayliff Street, Whitechapel, London, born 16 Jan, bapt 13 Feb 1814. [E]

DUNCAN, ALEXANDER, of Ardownie, Angus, a church member QEC, 1743. [DCA.GD/EC/D10/2/3]

DUNCAN, Rev Dr ALEXANDER, minister of the QEC, from 1785 until 1795. [DCA:GD/EC/D10/1/1] [DCA.GD/EC/D10/2/2][E]

DUNCAN, CATHARINE, born 4 Feb., bap. 11 Feb. 1818, dau. of Peter Duncan, a mariner, born in Errol, Perthshire, and his wife Helen, dau. of Robert Boyd, a labourer in Mains, Dundee. [E]

DUNCAN, DAVID, merchant, church member, 1777, 1781. [DCA:GD/EC/D10/1/2][S]

DUNCAN, ELIZABETH SPENCE, dau of Thomas Duncan and Euphemia Greene, born 20 Oct, bapt 12 Nov 1815. [S]

DUNCAN, JAMES, a merchant in Dundee, 1727. [ECD]; his widow a pensioner in 1742. [DCA.GD/EC/D10/2/1]

DUNCAN, JAMES, a schoolmaster and church member, 1764. [DCA.GD/EC/DIO/2/1]

DUNCAN, JAMES, a church member, 1811. [DCA:GD/EC/D10/1/1]

DUNCAN, JAMES, and Betty Williamson, both in Dundee, were married 25 Feb.1827. [E]

DUNCAN, PETER, son of James Duncan, a Private in the Royal Engineers, and Sophia his wife, born 1 Apr, bapt 14 Apr 1814. [S]

DUNCAN, ROBERT, a white ironsmith, member QEC, 1776, 1784. [DCA:GD/EC/D10/1/1] [DCA.GD/EC/D10/2/2][E]

DUNCAN, THOMAS, 1st son of Thomas Duncan, a Private of the 8th Royal Veteran Battalion, born in Raphoe, County Donegal, Ireland, and his wife Catherine, dau of William Duncan farmer in Carndonagh, County Londonderry, Ireland, born 31 Aug, bapt 1 Sept 1820. [E]

DUNCAN, ..., of Ardownie, Angus, in Dundee, 1727. [ECD]; 1743 [DCA.GD/EC/DIO/2/1]

DUNCAN, Mr, member QEC, 1776. [DCA:GD/EC/D10/1/1]

DUNLOP, BETTY, dau of James Dunlop and Betty his wife, born 4 Nov bapt 2 Nov 1813. [S]

DUNN, JANET, pensioner, 1743. [DCA.GD/EC/D10/2/1]

DUNN, JANET, 1st dau of John Dunn, a Private of the 79th Regiment, born in Ayr, and his wife Mary, dau of James Bruce weaver in Dunblane, Perthshire, born 1st March, bapt 2 March 1811. [E]

DUNN, ..., and his wife, members of the Scots Episcopal Chapel, Castle Street, Dundee, 1824/1828. [DCA.GD.EC.D10.1/3]

DUNN, JOHN, merchant, member of the QEC, 1776, 1777. [DCA:GD/EC/D10/1/1] [DCA.GD/EC/D10/2/2][E]

DUNNING, ALEXANDER, son of Matthew Dunning and Isabella his wife, born 3 Feb, bapt 20 Feb 1814. [S]

DURHAM, BETTY. church member, 1764. [DCA.GD/EC/DIO/2/1]

DURHAM, Mrs NELLY, church member, 1746. [DCA.GD/EC/D10/2/1]

DURHAM, Mrs, church member, 1746. [DCA.GD/EC/D10/2/1]

DURHAM, Mr, church member, 1758. [DCA.GD/EC/D10/2/2][E]

DUTTON, Mrs, a member of the Scots Episcopal Chapel, Castle Street, Dundee, 1824. [DCA.GD.EC.D10.1/3]

DYE, JAMES, son of John Dye and his wife Mary, born 20 Feb., bap. 3 Apl. 1817. [S]

EDWARDS, AGNES, a pensioner, aged 70 in 1818. [S][DARC.GD.EC.D10.1/2]

EDWARDS, HENRIETTA, a pensioner aged 66 in 1818. [S][DARC.GD.EC.D10.1/2]

EDWARDS, H., a member of the Scots Episcopal Chapel, Castle Street, Dundee, 1824. among the 'poor of St Paul's 1830' [DCA.GD.EC.D10.1/3]

EGLETON, JOHN, born 4 Feb., bap. 13 Feb. 1820, first son of Thomas Egleton, a cooper born in Sunderland, County Durham, England, and his wife Comb, dau. of David Grant, a weaver in Dundee. [E]

ELDER, BARBARA, 5th dau of John Elder porter, born in Tillon parish, and his wife Agnes Martin, dau of James Martin a weaver, born in Invergowrie, Perthshire, born 7 Feb, bapt 11 Feb 1809. [E]

ELDER, GRAHAM GOURLAY, 4th son of John Elder porter, born in Tillon parish, and his wife Agnes Martin, dau. of James Martin a weaver, born in Invergowrie, Perthshire, born 17 Feb, bapt 23 Feb 1812. [E]

ELDER, JAMES, pensioner, 1739. [DCA.GD/EC/DIO/2/1]

ELDER, JOHN, church member, 1811. [DCA: GD/EC/D10/1/1]

ELLESS, PETER, son of Peter Elless and Maria his wife, born 19 Feb, bapt 29 Feb 1812. [S]

ELLETT, AGNES WATSON, born 23 Dec.1819, bap. 20 Jan.1820, first dau. of William Ellett, a merchant born in Dundee, and his wife Elizabeth dau. of the late Duncan Watson, a baker in London. [E]

ELLETT, WILLIAM, a merchant, and Elizabeth Watson, both in Dundee, were married 18 Mar.1818. [E]

ELLETT, WILLIAM WEBSTER, born 13 Dec. 1818, bap. 7 Feb. 1819, first son of William Ellett, a merchant born in Dundee, and his wife Elizabeth, dau. of George Mew, a mariner, born in Poole, Hampshire, England. [E]

ELLICE, Miss, a member of the Scots Episcopal Chapel, Castle Street, Dundee, 1824. [DCA.GD.EC.D10.1/3]

EMERY, BELL, dau of Robert Emery and Margaret his wife, bapt 29 Dec 1811. [S]

EMERY, CHARLES, son of Robert Emery and Margaret his wife, born 7 Aug, bapt 14 Aug 1814. [S]

ERSKINE, CHRISTIAN, a spinster in Monifieth, Angus, married Charles Stirling a bachelor in Cadder, Lanarkshire, at the house of Thomas Erskine, Linlathen, Angus, 14 Oct. 1817. [S]

ERSKINE, JAMES, vestryman, 1814, 1816. [S][DCA: GD/EC/D10.1/2]

EWING, ROBERT, born 15 July, bapt. 14 July, 4th son of Alexander Ewing, a labourer, born in Kinglassie, Fife, and his wife Agnes, dau. of John McCulloch, a labourer in Dungannon, County Tyrone, Ireland. [E]

EVANS, SAMUEL, son of William Evans and Helen his wife, born 10 Nov. bapt. 6 Dec. 1812. [S]

EVANS, WILLIAM, church member, 1764. [DCA.GD/EC/DIO/2/1]

EWART, DAVID, son of David Ewart and his wife Eliza, born 22 Dec 1811, bapt. 12 Jan 1812. [S]

EWART, ELIZABETH GEORGIANA, dau of David Ewart and his wife Eliza, born 15 Dec 1813, bapt. 6 Feb 1814. [S]

EWART, JAMES ALEXANDER MITCHELL, son of David Ewart and his wife Eliza, born 9 July, bapt. 23 July 1815. [S]

FACHNEY, ANNE LOUISA, dau of George Fachney and Louisa his wife, born 12 Aug. bapt. 24 Sept. 1815. [S]

FAIRWEATHER, ROBERT, son of Robert Fairweather and Jane Lyon, born 15 Oct. bapt. 30 Oct. 1814. [S]

FARQUHARSON, ALEXANDER, 5th son of Innes Farquharson, a cabinet-maker, born in Glamis, Angus, and his wife Isabel, dau. of Peter Waller porter in Dundee, born 24 Sept. bapt. 2 Oct. 1814. [E]

FARQUHARSON, CHARLES, a watchmaker in Dundee, vestryman of the QEC, 1757. [DCA:GD/EC/D10/1/1] [DCA.GD/EC/D10/2/2][E]

FARQUHARSON, DAVID, church member, 1743. [DCA.GD/EC/D10/2/3]

FARQUHARSON, DAVID, born 21 Sep. bapt. 6 Oct. 1816, son of Innes Farquharson, a cabinet maker, born in Glamis, Angus, and his wife Isabel Waller, dau. of Peter Waller, a porter in Dundee. [E]

FARQUHARSON, DAVID, born 30 Sep. bapt. 12 Oct. 1817, son of Innes Farquharson, a cabinet maker, born in Glamis, Angus, and his wife Isabel Waller, dau. of Peter Waller, a porter in Dundee. [E]

FARQUHARSON, ELSPETH, 3rd dau of Innes Farquharson, a cabinet-maker, born in Glamis, Angus, and his wife Isabel, dau of Peter Waller a porter in Dundee, born 28 June, bapt. 12 July 1812. [E]

FARQUHARSON, ISABEL, dau. of James Farquharson, a Private in the 2nd Battalion of the 79th Regiment. and Margaret his wife, born 9 Dec. 1812, bapt. 10 Jan. 1813. [S]

FARQUHARSON, JAMES, born 30 Mar. bapt. 9 Apr. 1820, son of Innes Farquharson, a cabinet maker, born in Glamis, Angus, and his wife Isabel Waller, dau. of Peter Waller, a porter in Dundee. [E]

FARQUHARSON, MARY, a pensioner aged 74 in 1818. [S] [DARC.GD.EC.D10.1/2]

FARQUHARSON, PAUL, church member, 1743. [DCA.GD/EC/DIO/2/1]; a vintner, and vestryman of the QEC, 1757. [DCA:GD/EC/D10/1/1] [DCA.GD/EC/D10/2/2][E]

FARQUHARSON, ROBERT, and Catharine Campbell, both in Dundee, were married 10 July 1815. [E]

FARQUHARSON, WALTER, son of David Farquharson and Mary Kid, born 28 June, bapt. 4 July 1813. [S]

FARQUHARSON, Dr WILLIAM, vestryman of the QEC, 1764, 1772; member 1776. [DCA:GD/EC/D10/1/1]

FARQUHARSON, WILLIAM, 4th son of Innes Farquharson, a cabinet-maker, born in Glamis, Angus, and his wife Isabel, dau. of Peter Waller, porter in Dundee, born 23 April, bapt. 23 April 1810. [E]

FERGUSON, ALEXANDER BELSHES, born 20 Dec. 1828, bapt. 4 Jan. 1829, 2nd son of John Ferguson, an Excise officer, born in Perth, and his wife Jane, dau. of James Cameron, overseer at the bleachfield at Tilloch. [E]

FERGUSON, JANET, a spinster in Dundee, and William Mason, a labourer in Dundee, a widower, were married in St Paul's Chapel, Dundee, 5 Sep. 1824. [S]

FERRIER, ALEXANDER SCOTT, born 8 Oct. bapt. 29 Nov. 1829, 1st son of John Ferrier, a seaman, born in Dundee, and his wife Elizabeth, dau. of Thomas Ross, a Private soldier of the 79th Regiment of Foot. [E]

FIFE, ALEXANDER, son of David Fife, a merchant in Dundee, was bapt. 14 Apr. 1724. [BN]

FIFE, DAVID, son of David Fife, a merchant in Dundee, was bapt. 13 Jan. 1725. [BN]

FIFE, JAMES, son of David Fife, a merchant in Dundee, was bapt. 7 Nov. 1722. [BN]

FIN, ALEXANDER, a weaver, church member, 1777. [DCA.GD/EC/D10/1/2][S]

FINN, ELIZABETH, a pensioner aged 72 in 1818. [S][DARC.GD.EC.D10.1/2]

FINN, JAMES, a member of the Scots Episcopal Chapel, Castle Street, Dundee, 1824. [DCA.GD.EC.D10.1/3]

FIN, JAMES, a weaver, church member, 1764, 1777, 1781. [DCA:GD/EC/D10/1/2][S]

FIN, PATRICK, weaver, church member, 1777, 1781. [DCA:GD/EC/D10/1/2][S]

FINDLAY, ALEXANDER GEORGE, son of Charles Findlay and his wife Margaret Anne, born 28 Mar. bapt. 7 May 1815. [S]

FINLAY, ALEXANDER, born 29 Feb. bapt. 19 Apr. 1824, 1st son. of Roderick Finlay, a cooper in Broughty Ferry, Angus, born in Dundee, and his wife Janet, dau. of Alexander Annandale, a brewer in Broughty Ferry, Angus. [E]

FINLAY, ANDREW, pensioner, 1739. [DCA.GD/EC/DIO/2/1]

FINLAY, ANN, a spinster in Dundee, and James McDonald, a bachelor in Dundee, were married in her father's house in Thorter Row, Dundee, 19 Nov 1828. [S]

FINDLAY, CATHERINE, dau. of Joseph Findlay, a Private in the Forfarshire [Angus] Militia, and Margaret his wife, born 27 Feb. bapt. 12 Mar. 1812. [S]

FINDLAY, CHARLES, 1st son of Charles Findlay, a Private of the Forfarshire [Angus] Militia, born in Forfar, Angus, and his wife Mary, dau. of John Robinson, a blacksmith, late of Dundee, born 1 Dec. 1809, bapt. 13 Dec. 1809. [E]

FINDLAY, CHARLES WEMYSS BROWN, son of Charles Findlay and his wife Margaret Anne, born 2 Dec. 1812, bapt. 24 Jan 1813. [S]

FINDLAY, CHARLES, born 22 Aug. bapt. 3 Oct. 1819, second son of Charles Findlay, a weaver born in Forfar, Angus, and his wife Mary, dau. of John Robinson, a blacksmith, late of Dundee. [E]

FINLAY, DAVID, born 24 June, bapt. 8 July 1827, 2nd son of Robert Finlay, a sailor, born in Dundee, and his wife Harriet, dau. of Daniel Lambird, a waterman in Gravesend, Kent, England. [E]

FINLAY, HANNAH, born 12 Mar. bap. 29 Apr. 1824, 1st son. of Roderick Finlay, a cooper in Broughty Ferry, Angus, born in Dundee, and his wife Janet, dau. of Alexander Annandale, a brewer in Broughty Ferry, Angus. [E]

FINLAY, JANE, born 11 Sep. bapt. 19 Oct. 1826, 1st son. of Roderick Finlay, a cooper in Broughty Ferry, Angus, born in Dundee, and his wife Janet, dau. of Alexander Annandale, a brewer in Broughty Ferry, Angus. [E]

FINLAY, MARY JANE LAMBIRD, born 11 Nov. bapt. 22 Nov. 1829, daughter of Robert Finlay, a sailor, born in Dundee, and his wife Harriet, dau. of Daniel Lambird, a waterman in Gravesend, Kent, England. [E]

FINDLAY, ROBERT, a slater, church member, 1777. [DCA.GD/EC/D10/1/2][S]

FINLAYSON, JAMES, pensioner, 1739. [DCA.GD/EC/DIO/2/1]

FINLAYSON, MARY, dau. of George Finlayson and Jane Graham, born 25 Oct. 1816, bapt. 5 Jan. 1817. [S]

FINLAYSON, THOMAS, a jeweller in Paisley, Renfrewshire, and Isobel Bayne in Dundee, were married on 3 Dec. 1808, witness Charles Bayne. [E]

FINN, ELIZABETH, a pensioner aged 72 in 1818. [S][DCA.GD.EC.D10.1/2]

FINN, JAMES, a member of the Scots Episcopal Chapel, Castle Street, Dundee, 1824. [DCA.GD.EC.D10.1/3]

FINN, WILLIAM, a member of the Scots Episcopal Chapel, Castle Street, Dundee, 1824. [DCA.GD.EC.D10.1/3]

FLEMING, TILLY, dau. of John Fleming and Jane Stuart, born 22 Mar. bapt. 1 Apl. 1817. [S]

FLETCHER, Major, member of the QEC, 1776. [DCA:GD/EC/D10/1/1]

FLETCHER, ..., of Lindertis, [DCA.GD/EC/D10/2/2][E]

FLIGHT, Mrs, widow of a hammerman, [a smith] a pensioner aged 76 in 1818. [S][DCA.GD.EC.D10.1/2]

FOLDS, THOMAS, son of William Folds and Catherine his wife, born 20 May, bapt. 28 June 1812. [S]

FOORD, HELEN, pensioner, 1739. [DCA.GD/EC/DIO/2/1]

FORBES, DAVID, son of Robert Forbes and Margaret his wife, born 18 Oct. bapt. 31 Oct. 1813. [S]

FORBES, ELIZABETH, dau. of John Forbes and Ellen Ireland, born 18 July, bapt. 15 Oct. 1815. [S]

FORBES, JOHN, son of Robert Forbes and Margaret his wife, born 24 Apr. bapt. 5 May 1816. [S]

FORD, MARGARET, dau. of John Ford and Anne Forester, bapt. 12 Feb. 1811. [S]

FOREMAN, JOHN, pensioner, 1743. [DCA.GD/EC/D10/2/1]

FORRESTER, DAVID, 5th son of John Forrester, labourer at the Mill of Balmuir, Angus, born in Dundee, and his wife Elizabeth, dau. of David Hutchison, labourer in Strathmartin, Angus, born 4 Oct. bapt. 28 Oct. 1810. [E]

FORRESTER, JOHN, pensioner, 1740. [DCA.GD/EC/DIO/2/1]

FORRESTER, JOHN, church member, 1811. [DCA:GD/EC/D10]

FORRESTER, ROBERT, pensioner, 1743. [DCA.GD/EC/D10/2/1]

FORSYTH, KITTY ANNE, dau. of William Forsyth and Anne his wife, born 2 Dec. bapt. 31 Dec. 1815. [S]

FOSTER, Miss, member of the QEC, 1776. [DCA:GD/EC/D10/1/1]

FOTHERINGHAM, DAVID, son of James Fotheringham, a merchant in Dundee, was bapt. 15 Feb. 1725, Archibald Fotheringham of Drumlochie and John Strachan, a merchant, were godfathers, while Mrs Helen Miln, dau. of the laird of Milnefield in Perthshire, was godmother. [BN]. [During the Jacobite Rising of 1715 he was the Governor of Dundee.]

FOTHERINGHAM, JAMES, church member, 1758. [DCA.GD/EC/D10/2/2][E]

FOTHERINGHAM, ROBERT, son of James Fotheringham, a merchant in Dundee, was bapt. on 19 ... 1724, Robert Graham eldest son to the laird of Fintry and James Clephan, son of Colonel Clephan were godfathers, while Lady Balinshaw was godmother. [BN]

FOTHERINGHAM, Dr ROBERT, QEC committee member, 1757. [DCA:GD/EC/D10/1/1]

FOTHERINGHAM, THOMAS, of Powrie, 1758, member of the QEC, 1776. [DCA:GD/EC/D10/1/1] [DCA.GD/EC/D10/2/2][E]

FOTHERINGHAM, Mrs, church member, 1764. [DCA.GD/EC/DIO/2/1]

FOWLER, ROBERT, church member, 1743. [DCA.GD/EC/DIO/2/1; 2/3]

FRASER, CHARLES BASS, born 22 Jan. bapt. 8 Feb. 1829, 6th son of Alexander Fraser, a tailor, born in Inverness, and his wife Isabella, dau. of Peter Mackay, a shoemaker in Aberdeen. [E]

FRASER, ELIZABETH, dau. of Daniel Fraser and Janet his wife, born 8 Feb. bapt. 20 Feb 1814. [S]

FRASER, GEORGE, church member, 1781. [DCA.GD/EC/D10/1/2][S]

FRASER, JAMES, born 3 Jan. bapt. 28 Jan. 1821, 3rd son of Alexander Fraser, a flaxdresser, born in Aberdeen, and his wife Mary, dau. of William Thompson, a gardener in Aberdeen. [E]

FRASER, JOHN, a labourer, and Margaret Ambrose, both in Dundee, were married 30 July 1820. [E]

FULLARTON, Mrs ANNE, church member, 1746. [DCA.GD/EC/D10/2/1]

FULLARTON, GEORGE, church member, 1743. [DCA.GD/EC/DIO/2/1;2/3]

FYFFE, CRAIGIE, dau. of James Fyffe and Ellen his wife, born 3 Apr. bapt. 22 Aug. 1813. [S]

FYFFE, DAVID, minister of the Seagait Chapel, in Dundee, from 1743 until 1745. [ECD]

FYFFE, DAVID, of Drumgeith, Angus, church member, 1784. [DCA.GD/EC/D10/2/2][E]

FYFFE, DAVID, vestryman, 1802. [DCA.GD/EC/D10/1/2][S]

FYFFE, Major DAVID, of Logie, Dundee, a vestryman, 1825/1828/1830. [DCA.GD.EC.D10.1/3]

FYFFE, ELLEN, dau. of James Fyffe and Ellen his wife, born 15 Mar. bapt. 30 July 1815. [S]

FYFFE, JAMES, son of James Fyffe and Margaret Fike (?), born 24 Nov. bapt. 14 Dec. 1816. [S]

FYFFE, Mrs, among the 'poor of Mr Hetherton's congregation, 1830' [DCA.GD.EC.D10.1/3]

GALL, JOHN, church member, 1743. [DCA.GD/EC/DIO/2/1; 2/3]

GALLOW, ELIZABETH, dau. of Alexander Gallow and Elizabeth Anderson, born 20 Mar 1811, bapt. 2 Oct. 1814. [S]

GALLOWAY, ALEXANDER, 1st son of Frederic Galloway, a weaver, born in Dundee, and his wife Janet, dau. of Donald Robinson, a mariner in Dundee, born 22 Nov. bapt. 12 Dec 1813. [E]

GALLOWAY, JAMES, church member, 1764. [DCA.GD/EC/DIO/2/1]

GALLOWAY, PETER, church member, 1784. [DCA.GD/EC/D10/2/2][E]

GARDINER, EUPHEMIA, a spinster in Dundee, and James Mackenzie, bachelor in Dundee, were married in the vestry of St Paul's, Castle Street, Dundee, 3 June 1827. [S]

GARRIE, WILLIAM, a Corporal of the 62nd Regiment, a bachelor in Dundee, and Ann Webster, a spinster in Dundee, were married in the vestry of the Episcopal Chapel, Castle Street, Dundee, 1824. [DCA.GD.EC.D10.1/3]

GAULD, JAMES, a blacksmith in Dundee, and Christian Beugie, a widow in Dundee, were married, 13 June 1823. [S]

GEARY, EUPHEMIA, dau. of John Geary and Agnes his wife, born 18 Dec. 1812, bapt. 10 Jan. 1813. [S]

GEDDIE, DAVID, son of David Geddie and Elizabeth Janan, born 2 Sept. bapt. 13 Sept. 1812. [S]

GEEKIE, Mrs, member QEC, 1776, 1784. [DCA:GD/EC/D10/1/1] [DCA.GD/EC/D10/2/2][E]

GIB, BARBARA, dau. of Robert Gib tailor in Dundee, was bap. 17 July 1726. [BN]

GIBB, ELIZA, church member, 1764. [DCA.GD/EC/DIO/2/1]

GIBB, JAMES, church member, 1743. [DCA.GD/EC/DIO/2/1; 2/3]

GIB, JOHN, son of Robert Gib tailor in the Nethergait, Dundee was bapt. 13 July 1723. [BN]

GIBB, JOHN, a member of the Scots Episcopal Chapel, Castle Street, Dundee, 1824. [DCA.GD.EC.D10.1/3]

GIBB, MARY, dau of John Gibb and his wife Mary, born 26 July, bapt. 31 July 1814. [S]

GIBB, PATRICK, church member, 1777. [DCA.GD/EC/D10/1/2][S]

GIB, ROBERT, in Dundee, 1727. [ECD]; church member, 1743. [DCA.GD/EC/DIO/2/1; 2/3]

GIB, ROBERT, church member, 1764. [DCA.GD/EC/DIO/2/1]

GIBB, ..., a member QEC, 1776. [DCA:GD/EC/D10/1/1]

GIBBONS, GEORGE, son of George Gibbons and Jane his wife, born 23 Dec. 1814, bapt. 21 May 1815. [S]

GIBSON, GEORGE, born 2 Aug. bapt. 20 Aug 1821, 2nd son of Joseph Gibson, born in Monaghan, Ireland, a Private of the 8th Royal Veteran Battalion, and his wife Elizabeth, dau. of Robert Sneddon, late of Tullycorbet, County Monaghan, a Private soldier. [E]

GIBSON, JOHN JAMES, born 1 July. bapt. 21 July 1822, 3rd son of Joseph Gibson, born in Monaghan, Ireland, a Private of the 8th Royal Veteran Battalion, and his wife Elizabeth, dau. of Robert Sneddon, late of Tullycorbet, County Monaghan, a Private soldier. [E]

GIBSON, MARGARET, 4th dau of Robert Gibson, a labourer, born in Stonekirk, Wigtonshire, and his wife Margaret, dau. of William Little, farmer in Dalbeattie, Dumfries-shire, born 26 July, bapt. 8 Aug 1819. [E]

GIBSON, SAMUEL, son of Samuel Gibson and Margaret Lawson, born 3 June, bapt. 23 July 1815. [S]

GILCHRIST, DAVID, born 6 Aug. bapt. 19 Aug. 1827, 1st son of James Gilchrist, a Private in the Rifle Brigade, born in Belfast, Ireland, and his wife Mary, dau. of Robert Mitchell, a gardener in Aberdeen. [E]

GILCHRIST, ISABELLA, dau of Alexander Gilchrist private of the 79th Regiment of Foot and Jane his wife, born 4 Jan, bapt 5 Feb 1812. [S]

GILCHRIST, Mrs, a member of the Scots Episcopal Chapel, Castle Street, Dundee, 1824. [DCA.GD.EC.D10.1/3]

GILLES, Mrs, relict of Thomas Gilles, a pensioner, 1746. [DCA.GD/EC/D10/2/1]

GILLESPIE, JAMES, bachelor in Dundee, and Margaret Crooks, a spinster in Dundee, were married in the house of Rev. H. Horsley, Magdalene Yard, Perth Road, Dundee, 22 Jan. 1836. []

GILROY, GEORGE, son of Alexander Gilroy and Elizabeth his wife, born 9 Feb bapt 6 Mar 1815. [S]

GIRKINS, MARY ROGER, born 22 Aug., bap. 23 Sep. 1827, 3rd dau. of Peter Girkins, a sugar baker, born in Bremen, Germany, and his wife Frances, dau. of Thomas Goddard, a labourer in Balcolmstead, Hertfordshire, England. [E]

GLASGOW, ALEXANDER, a soldier in the 47th Regiment of Foot, and Margaret Reed, were married 13 July 1814. [E]

GODDARD, AGNES, 1st dau of Jeffrey Goddard, a Corporal of the 39th Regiment of Foot, born in Lynn, Norfolk, England, and his wife Margaret, dau of James Leuchars, a gardener in Dundee, born 26 May, bapt 3 June 1810. [E]

GOLDMAN, BARBARA, dau of James Goldman a minister in Dundee, was bapt 13 Aug 1723, godfather was George Rait MD in Dundee, and godmothers were Barbara Rait, dau of William Rait minister of Monikie, Angus, and Barbara Goldman, dau of Alexander Goldman in Dundee. [BN]

GOLDMAN, JAMES, minister of St Paul's, Dundee, from 1704 until 1727; also, the Seagait Chapel, in Dundee, from 1727 until 1742; in Dundee, 1727. [ECD]

GOLDMAN, JAMES, son of James Goldman minister in Dundee, was bapt 1 Apr 1725, godfathers were Dr George Rait and George Dempster, a merchant in Dundee, with the wife of Dr Rait as godmother. [BN]

GOODFELLOW, ELIZABETH, dau of William Goodfellow and Clementina Jackson, born 4 Sept 1809, bapt 7 June 1812. [S]

GOODLAD, JAMES, son of James Goodlad and Betty Grant, born 2 June, bapt 5 July 1813. [S]

GOODLET, BARBARA, 3rd dau of James Goodlet weaver, born in Kirriemuir, and his wife Angus, Jane, dau of the late John Gibson weaver in Murroes, Angus, born 19 Sept, bapt 13 Oct 1810. [E]

GOODLET, GEORGE, 2nd son of James Goodlet, a weaver, born in Kirriemuir, Angus, and his wife Jane, dau of the late John Gibson, a weaver in Murroes, Angus, born 20 Feb, bapt 25 Feb 1810. [E]

GOODLET, JAMES, born 12 Feb., bap. 3 Mar. 1816, son of James Goodlet, a weaver and native of Kirriemuir, Angus, and his wife Janet Gibson, dau. of John Gibson a weaver in Murroes, Angus. [E]

GOODLET, JANET, 4th dau of James Goodlet, a weaver, born in Kirriemuir, Angus, and his wife Jane, dau of the late John Gibson weaver in Murroes, Angus, born 9 Mar, bapt 2 April 1812. [E]

GOODLET, WILLIAM, 4th son of James Goodlet, a weaver, born in Kirriemuir, Angus, and his wife Jane, dau of the late John Gibson weaver in Murroes, Angus, born 12 June, bapt 21 June 1821. [E]

GORDON, MARGARET, dau. of Alexander Gordon and Jane Fraser, born 4 Sep. 1816, bap. 5 Jan. 1817. [S]

GORDON, MARGARET, a spinster in Dundee, and John Monro, a widower in Dundee, married in the house of James Robb, Castle Street, Dundee 4 July 1831. [S]

GORDON, ROBERT, son of Robert Gordon and Margaret Blain, bapt. 12 Feb 1811. [S]

GORDON, WILLIAM, son of John Gordon and Elizabeth Wallace, born 6 Dec 1815, bapt 25 Feb 1816. [S]

GORDON, Mrs, member QEC, 1776. [DCA:GD/EC/D10/1/1]

GORRIE, JOHN, a bachelor in Ferryport-on-Craig, Fife, married Agnes Marshall, a spinster in Ferryport-on-Craig, at the house of Mrs Addison, High Street, Dundee, 31 Dec. 1820. [S]

GRAHAME, ALEXANDER, son of Walter Grahame, a merchant in Dundee, was bapt 11 Dec 1722, Walter's brothers Alexander and John Grahame were godfathers and Christian Graham their sister was godmother. [BN]

GRAHAM, ALEXANDER, of Duntroon, Angus, a church member, 1784. [DCA.GD/EC/D10/2/2][E]

GRAHAME, ANN, dau of David Grahame in Duntrune, Angus, was bapt 28 June 1726, godfather was James Ramsay, a merchant in Dundee, while the Lady Dowager of Dundee and the Lady Fintry were godmothers. [BN]

GRAHAM, ANN, of Duntrune, Angus, a spinster, died 24 Feb 1809. [E]

GRAHAME, CHARLES DAVID, son of David Grahame in Duntrune, Angus, was bapt at Duntrune, 27 Mar 1723, godfathers were the Master of Gray and John Grahame, merchant in Dundee, while the Mistress of Gray was godmother. [BN]

GRAHAME, CLEMENTINA, dau of David Grahame in Duntrune, Angus, was bapt 3 Sept 1724, godfather was Alexander Grahame, a merchant in Dundee, with Lady Dundee and her dau Mrs Alison Grahame being godmothers. [BN]

GRAHAM, DAVID, in Dundee, 1743. [ECD]

GRAHAM, DAVID, of Mayfield, Dundee, son of Charles Graham, a merchant and his wife Janet Yeaman, born 1800, died 5 July 1809. [E]

GRAHAME, ELIZABETH, dau of Walter Grahame, a merchant in Dundee, was bapt 5 Feb 1724, godfather was John Grahame younger brother of the said Walter Grahame, with Mrs White and her dau, wife of Provost Guthrie, being godmothers. [BN]

GRAHAME, ELIZABETH, dau of John Grahame, a merchant in Dundee, was bapt 30 July 1725, godfather was John Grahame his brother, and godmothers were the wife of ....Wallace of Craigie, Dundee, and the wife of Milnhill. [BN]

GRAHAME, GEORGE, son of Walter Graham, a merchant in Dundee, was bapt 19 Dec 1725, godfathers were George Dempster and George Ramsay merchants in Dundee, with Mrs Grisel Grahame sister german to Walter Graham as godmother. [BN]

GRAHAM, GEORGE, of Flemington, Angus, a merchant in Dundee, vestryman, QEC, 1757; vestryman 1764; 1776; 1785. [DCA:GD/EC/D10/1/1] [DCA.GD/EC/D10/2/2][E]

GRAHAM, Mrs GRIZEL, church member, 1758. [DCA.GD/EC/D10/2/2][E]

GRAHAM, JAMES, of Methie, Angus, QEC committee, 1757; vestryman 1764, 1768; 1776. [DCA:GD/EC/D10/1/1] [DCA.GD/EC/D10/2/2][E] [DCA.GD/EC/D10/2/2][E][a Jacobite in 1745]

GRAHAM, JOHN, 1st dau of Charles Graham of Mayfield, Dundee, a merchant, born in Powrie, Murroes, Angus, and his wife Janet, dau of James Yeaman of Affleck, Angus, born 29 Mar, bapt 14 April 1809. [E]

GRAHAME, JOHN, and ROBERT, twin sons of David Grahame, a vintner in Couttie's Wynd, Dundee, were bapt 24 June 1722, witnesses were James Young, a surgeon apothecary and ..... Westhall. [BN]

GRAHAM, MARGARET SMITH, born 14 Mar., bap. 8 Apr. 1821, 1st dau. of Walter Graham, a weaver, born in Perth, and his wife Isabell, dau. of Robert Bruce a labo

urer in Dundee. [E]

GRAHAM, ROBERT, in Dundee, 1727. [ECD]

GRAHAM, ROBERT, of Fintry, Angus, in Dundee, 1727. [ECD]

GRAHAM, ROBERT, of Fintry, Angus, 1784. [DCA.GD/EC/D10/2/2][E]

GRAHAME, WILLIAM, a weaver, and Isabella Bruce, both in Dundee, were married 18 Sep. 1817. [E]

GRAHAM, Lady, of Fintry, Angus, church member, 1764. [DCA.GD/EC/DIO/2/1]

GRAHAM, ..., of Fintry, Angus, member QEC, 1776.

[DCA:GD/EC/D10/1/1]

GRAHAM, Mrs, of Methie, Angus, church member, 1784. [DCA.GD/EC/D10/2/2][E]

GRAHAM, Mrs, of Dalmuir, Angus, member QEC, 1810. [DCA.GD/EC/D10/1/2][S]

GRANT, BETSEY, dau of David Grant and Mary his wife, born 19 Feb. bapt 20 Mar 1815. [S]

GRANT, CHARLES, minister of the Qualified Chapel in Dundee, from 1795 until 1807. [QEC]

GRASSEY, JAMES, born 3 Feb., bap. 5 June 1825, 1st son of John Grassey, a flax dresser, born in Laurencekirk, Kincardineshire, and his wife Elizabeth, dau. of John Welsh, a shoemaker in Dundee. [E]

GRAY, AGNES, dau of John Gray and Agnes his wife, born 31 Mar, bapt 25 Apr 1815. [S]

GRAY, ALEXANDER, son of Charles Gray and Mary his wife, born 18 Sep 1814, bapt 15 Jan 1815. [S]

GRAY, ANDREW, a brewer or maltman in Dundee, 1727.[ECD]; a pensioner, 1740, 1742. [DCA.GD/EC/DIO/2/1]

GRAY, CATHERINE LAWSON, dau of Alexander Gray and Catherine Dixon, born 6 May, bapt 12 June 1814. [S]

GRAY, EDWARD, son of Margaret Gray a single woman in Dundee, dau of John Gray merchant in Forfar, Angus, born 26 Oct, bapt 9 Dec 1810. [E]

GRAY, ELIZABETH, 2nd dau of James Gray, a drummer of the 55th Regiment of Foot, born in Banff, Banffshire, and his wife Margaret Hay, dau of John Hay, a rope and sail maker in Dundee, born 7 Dec, bapt 21 Dec 1810. [E]

GRAY, ELIZABETH, 3rd dau of James Gray, a private of the 55th Regiment of Foot, born in Banff, Banffshire, and his wife Margaret Hay, dau of John Hay, a rope and sail maker in Dundee, born 31 Aug, bapt 13 Sept 1812. [E]

GRAY, HETHERTON, born 3 Apl., bap. 18 Apl. 1819, child of James Gray, late a private in the 55th Regiment of Foot now a pensioner, and his wife Margaret, dau. of John Hay, a rope and sail-maker in Dundee, [E]

GRAY, or SCOTT, ISABEL, a widow in Dundee, and David Mitchell, a bachelor in Dundee, were married in her house in Perth Road, Dundee, 4 Mar. 1828. [S]

GRAY, JAMES, in Dundee, 1727. [ECD]; surgeon, church member, 1743. [DCA.GD/EC/DIO/2/1; 2/3]

GRAY, JOHN, son of James Gray in Cottarton of Craigie, Angus, bapt 27 June 1725. [BN]

GRAY, JOHN, a merchant, member QEC, 1776, vestryman 1801. [DCA:GD/EC/D10/1/1]

GRAY, JOHN, a vestryman, 1816/1817/1818/1825/1830; and his wife, members of the Scots Episcopal Chapel, Castle Street, Dundee, 1824/1828; a merchant, 1825. [S][DCA.GD.EC.D10.1/2/3]

GRAY, MARGARET, born 3 Apl., bap. 18 Apl. 1819, dau. of James Gray, late a Private in the 55th Regiment of Foot now a pensioner, and his wife Margaret, dau. of John Hay a rope and sail-maker in Dundee, [E]

GRAY, MARTHA, born 20 May, bap. 14 June 1818, fifth dau. of Alexander Gray, a travelling merchant, born in Dundee, and his wife Sophia, dau. of John Young, a labourer in Dundee. [E]

GRAY, MARY, a spinster in Dundee, married William Ducat, a bachelor in Kinnettles, Angus, at the house of Mrs Gray, Tay Square, Dundee, on 29 Mar. 1819. [S]

GRAY, Miss M., a member of the Scots Episcopal Chapel, Castle Street, Dundee, 1824. [DCA.GD.EC.D10.1/3]

GRAY, Miss N., a member of the Scots Episcopal Chapel, Castle Street, Dundee, 1824. [GD.EC.D10.1/3]

GRAY, PATRICK, a surgeon, church member, 1750. [DCA.GD/EC/DIO/2/1]

GRAY, ROBERT, son of John Gray and Agnes his wife, born 26 Oct, bapt 19 Nov 1811. [S]

GRAY, WILLIAM, of Balledgarno, in Perthshire, 1785. [DCA.GD/EC/D10/2/2][E]

GRAY, WILLIAM, son of John Gray and Agnes his wife, born 18 Feb, bapt 13 Mar 1814. [S]

GRAY, Lady, church member, 1758. [DCA.GD/EC/D10/2/2][E]

GRAY, Mr, member QEC, 1776. [DCA:GD/EC/D10/1/1]

GREEN, ISABELLA, dau of David Green and Isabell his wife, born 4 Sept, bapt 13 Sept 1812. [S]

GREEN, Mr, member QEC, 1776. [DCA:GD/EC/D10/1/1]

GREENHILL, ALEXANDER, merchant, church member, 1764, 1777, 1781. [DCA:GD/EC/D10/1/2][S][DCA.GD/EC/DIO/2/1]

GREENHILL, CHARLES, merchant, vestryman, 1802; 1810. [DCA.GD/EC/D10/1/2][S]

GREENHILL, GEORGE, son of Patrick Greenhill in Dundee, bapt 19 Dec 1722. [BN]

GREENHILL, HELEN, dau of Patrick Greenhill of Banchrie, Perthshire, bapt 25 Feb 1724. [BN]

GREENHILL, JOHN, church member, 1764. [DCA.GD/EC/DIO/2/1]

GREENHILL, MARY, dau of Charles Greenhill and Anne Sturrock, born 7 Apr bapt 8 Aug 1812. [S]

GREENHILL, Mrs, church member, 1810. [DCA.GD/EC/D10/1/2][S]

GREIG, JAMES, son of James Greig and Mary his wife, born 12 Sept, bapt 25 Sept 1814. [S]

GREIG, THOMAS, a cotton printer in Bury, Lancashire, and Helen Watson, in Dundee, were married in the house of James Watson, Rosefield, Dundee, 6 Oct. 1834. [S]

GRIEVE, DAVID, son of William Grieve and his wife Janet, born 11 Jan., bap. 14 Jan. 1816. [S]

GREIVE, JOHN, son of George Greive and Margaret Ritchie, born 14 Dec 1814, bapt 8 Jan 1815. [S]

GRIEVE, MARGARET, dau. of David Grieve and Elizabeth his wife, born 27 Apl. bap. 12 May 1816. [S]

GREIVE, MARTHA, dau of William Greive and Jenny his wife, born 31 Oct, bapt 29 Nov 1812. [S]

GREIG, JOHN, pensioner, 1740. [DCA.GD/EC/DIO/2/1]

GRIEVE, ANDREW, pensioner, 1739. [DCA.GD/EC/DIO/2/1]

GRIG, ……., member QEC, 1776. [DCA:GD/EC/D10/1/1]

GRUBB, ANN STRACHAN, 4th dau of James Grubb, a salmon curer in Broughty Ferry, Angus, born in Brechin, Angus and his wife Hannah, dau of William Leach, born in Inworth, Essex, England, born 2 Feb, bapt 23 Feb 1809. [E]

GRUBB, WILLIAM SPEARS, 6th son of James Grubb, a salmon curer in Broughty Ferry, Angus, born in Brechin, Angus, and his wife Hannah, dau of William Leach, born in Inworth, Essex, England, born 15 July, bapt 1 Aug 1813. [E]

GRUBB, JOHN, son of John Grubb and Katherine his wife, born 17 Dec 1811, bapt 24 Mar 1812. [S]

GRUBB, PATRICK DALL, 7th son of James Grubb, a salmon curer in Broughty Ferry, Angus, born in Brechin, Angus, and his wife Hannah, dau of William Leach, born in Inworth, Essex, England, born 22 April, bapt 7 May 1812. [E]

GRUBB, WILLIAM SPEARS, 6th son of James Grubb, a salmon curer in Broughty Ferry, Angus, born in Brechin, Angus, and his wife Hannah, dau of William Leach, born in Inworth, Essex, England, born 25 May, bapt 13 June 1810. [E]

GRUBB, Captain, a church member, 1811. [DCA:GD/EC/D10/1/1]

GUILD, ALEXANDER, 1784. [DCA.GD/EC/D10/2/2][E]

GUNN, JAMES, born 3 Nov, 1815, bap. 25 Feb. 1816, son of John Gunn a travelling chapman, born in Canisby, Caithness, and his wife Christian Ross dau. of Daniel Ross a farmer in Fearn, Ross-shire. [E]

GUTHRIE, ALEXANDER, in Dundee, 1727. [ECD]; church member, 1743. [DCA.GD/EC/DIO/2/1]

GUTHRIE, ALEXANDER, church member, 1743. [DCA.GD/EC/DIO/2/1; 2/3] [a Jacobite in 1745]

GUTHRIE, CHARLES, member QEC, 1776, [DCA:GD/EC/D10/1/1]

GUTHRIE, CHARLES, of Taybank, Dundee, vestryman of the English Chapel in Dundee, 1808. [E]

GUTHRIE, CHRISTIAN, dau of John Guthrie merchant in Dundee, was bapt 7 Jan 1724. [BN]; church member, 1750. [DCA.GD/EC/DIO/2/1]

GUTHRIE, GEORGE, son of John Guthrie merchant in Dundee, was bapt 25 Jan 1725. [BN]

GUTHRIE, HELEN DOUGLAS, dau of John Guthrie and Anne his wife, born 16 Dec 1814, bapt 3 Jan 1815. [S]

GUTHRIE, HENRIETTA, pensioner, 1739. [DCA.GD/EC/DIO/2/1]

GUTHRIE, JAMES, son of John Guthrie merchant in Dundee, was bapt 3 Feb 1723. [BN]

GUTHRIE, JAMES, the younger, of Craigie, Dundee, QEC vestryman, 1758,1768, 1776, 1781, 1784. [DCA:GD/EC/D10/1/1] [DCA.GD/EC/D10/2/2][E]

GUTHRIE, JAMES, of Craigie, Dundee, a vestryman of the English Chapel, in Dundee, 1808.[E]

GUTHRIE, JAMES ALEXANDER, born 8 Sept., bap. 23 Sept. 1823, 1st son of David Charles Guthrie, a merchant in London, born in Craigie, Dundee, and his wife Jane Campbell, dau. of Sir John Hunter, Consul General in Spain. [E]

GUTHRIE, JOHN, in Dundee, 1727. [ECD]

GUTHRIE, JOHN, a merchant, church member, 1777, 1781. [DCA:GD/EC/D10/1/2][S]

GUTHRIE, MARGARET, dau. of David Guthrie and Elizabeth Gourlay, born 24 Dec. 1815, bap. 30 June 1816. [S]

GUTHRIE, PATRICK, a merchant in Brechin, Angus, and Margaret Watson in Dundee, were married 1 June 1829. [E]

GUTHRIE, ROBERT, a merchant in Dundee, 1727. [ECD]; church member, 1758. [DCA.GD/EC/D10/2/2][E]

GUTHRIE, ROBERT, a member of the Scots Episcopal Chapel, Castle Street, Dundee, 1824. [DCA.GD.EC.D10.1/3]

GUTHRIE, THOMAS, an apothecary in Dundee, 1727. [ECD]

GUTHRIE, THOMAS, of Clepington, in Dundee, 1727. [ECD]; 1743. [DCA.GD/EC/DIO/2/1]

GUTHRIE, WILLIAM, church member, 1781. [DCA.GD/EC/D10/1/2][S]

GUTHRIE, ..., of Craigie, Dundee, church member, 1743. [DCA.GD/EC/DIO/2/1]

GUTHRIE, ..., of Taybank, Dundee, a vestryman of the QEC, 1807. [DCA:GD/EC/D10/1/1]

GUTHRIE, Mrs, relict of David Guthrie, pensioner, 1739. [DCA.GD/EC/DIO/2/1]

HACKNEY, HELEN, a spinster in Aberlemno, Angus, married Thomas Coupar, a shipmaster in Dundee, a bachelor, at the house of David Caithness, a shipmaster in Dundee, 20 Dec. 1817. [S]

HACKNEY, ..., a vestryman, 1828. [E] [GD.EC.D10.1/1]

HAGGART, SUSAN, dau of James Haggart and Susan Milne, born 5 Apr, bapt 28 Aug 1814. [S]

HALIBURTON, Colonel JAMES, vestryman QEC, 1758, 1764. [DCA:GD/EC/D10/1/1] [DCA.GD/EC/D10/2/2][E]

HALIBURTON, JOHN, treasurer, 1757. [DCA.GD/EC/D10/2/2][E]

HALLIBURTON, ..., children of Thomas Halliburton, pensioners, 1745. [DCA.GD/EC/D10/2/1][Thomas Haliburton, a wright in Dundee, a Jacobite in 1745]

HALLIBURTON, Miss, church member, 1764. [DCA.GD/EC/DIO/2/1]

HAMILTON, GRIZZEL BROWN, 1st dau of John Hamilton, a cabinet-maker, born in Kingston, Jamaica, and his wife Isabella, dau of William Miller, a shoemaker in Dundee, born 1 Oct, bapt 12 Oct 1812. [E]

HAMILTON, GRAHAM, born 9 Oct., bap. 15 Oct. 1826, 3rd son of John Hamilton, a cabinet-maker, born in Kingston, Jamaica, and his wife Isabella Miller, dau. of the late William Miller, a shoemaker in Dundee. [E]

HAMILTON, JAMES, born 15 Feb., bap. 14 Feb. 1819, 2nd son of John Hamilton, a cabinet-maker, born in Kingston, Jamaica, and his wife Isabella Miller, dau. of the late William Miller, a shoemaker in Dundee. [E]

HAMILTON, JANE, born 29 June., bap. 30 June 1816, 2nd son of John Hamilton, a cabinet-maker, born in Kingston, Jamaica, and his wife Isabella Miller, dau. of the late William Miller, a shoemaker in Dundee. [E]

HAMILTON, JOHN MILLER, 1st son of John Hamilton, a cabinet-maker, born in Kingston, Jamaica, and his wife Isabella, dau of William Miller, a shoemaker in Dundee, born 24 May, bapt 5 June 1814. [E]

HAMILTON, MARGARET BROWN, born 15 Mar., bapt. 21 Mar. 1824, 4th dau. of John Hamilton, a cabinet-maker, born in Kingston, Jamaica, and his wife Isabella Miller, dau. of the late William Miller, a shoemaker in Dundee. [E]

HAMILTON, MARY LOCKHART, born 24 May., bapt. 30 May. 1821, 3rd dau. of John Hamilton, a cabinet-maker, born in Kingston, Jamaica, and his wife Isabella Miller, dau. of the late William Miller, a shoemaker in Dundee. [E]

HANTON, JOHN, 'blower', 1816/1817/1818. [S][DCA.GD.EC.D10.1/2]

HANTON, Mrs, a member of the Scots Episcopal Chapel, Castle Street, Dundee, 1824. among the 'poor of St Paul's 1830'. [DCA.GD.EC.D10.1/3]

HARLEY, DAVID, 5th son of Alexander Harley iron founder, born in Culross, Fife, and his wife Jane, dau of Charles Wright labourer, born in Incheidy, Perthshire, born 13 April, bapt. 28 April 1811. [E]

HARLEY, MARGERY, 1st dau of Alexander Harley, an iron founder, born in Culross, Fife, and his wife Jane Wright, dau of Charles Wright labourer, born in Incheidy, Perthshire, born 19 Feb, bapt. 5 Mar. 1809. [E]

HARRIS, WILLIAM CAMERON, son of James Harris, a private of the 69th Regiment, and Betty Lyon, born 23 Dec. 1811, bapt. 19 Jan. 1812. [S]

HAY, CHARLES, son of John Hay and Christian his wife, born 22 Oct. bapt. 18 Nov. 1815. [S]

HAY, DAVID, member QEC, 1776. [DCA:GD/EC/D10/1/1]

HAY, JAMES, son of Alexander Hay and Bell his wife, born April, bapt. 4 Dec. 1814. [S]

HAY, JOHN, church member, 1758. [DCA.GD/EC/D10/2/2][E]

HAY, LEWIS, a supervisor, vestryman QEC, 1771. [DCA:GD/EC/D10/1/1]

HAY, ROBERT, son of Robert Hay and Anne Gray, born 3 June, bapt. 13 Aug 1815. [S]

HAY, Mrs, a pensioner, 1746. [DCA.GD/EC/D10/2/1]

HAY, Miss, member of the QEC, 1776. [DCA:GD/EC/D10/1/1]

HAY, Mr, member of the QEC, 1776. [DCA:GD/EC/D10/1/1]

HAYWORTH, ROBERT, son of David Hayworth, Captain of the 21st Regiment, and Elizabeth his wife, born 28 Jan. bapt. 3 Feb. 1812. [S]

HAZEEL, ALEXANDER, born 30 Dec. 1825, bapt. 1 Feb. 1826, 3rd son of Alexander Hazeel, a weaver and manufacturer, born in Dundee, and his wife Sarah, dau. of John Rogers, farmer in Ipswich, Suffolk, England. [E]

HAZEEL, HAZEL, born 29 Dec. 1822, bap. 13 Jan. 1823, 2nd dau. of Alexander Hazeel, a weaver and manufacturer, born in Dundee, and his wife Sarah, dau. of John Rogers, farmer in Ipswich, Suffolk, England. [E]

HAZEEL, HENRY, born 1 June, bapt. 13 June 1824, 2nd son of Alexander Hazeel, a weaver and manufacturer, born in Dundee, and his wife Sarah, dau. of John Rogers, farmer in Ipswich, Suffolk, England. [E]

HAZEEL, JANET, born 29 Dec., bapt. 13 Jan. 1822, 2nd dau. of Alexander Hazeel, a weaver and manufacturer, born in Dundee, and his wife Sarah, dau. of John Rogers, farmer in Ipswich, Suffolk, England. [E]

HEGISON, Mrs, member of the QEC, 1776. [DCA:GD/EC/D10/1/1]

HENDERSON, DANIEL, a bachelor in Kettins, Angus married Elizabeth Archer, spinster in Kettins, at the Toll House of Auchterhouse, Angus, 12 June 1819. [S]

HENDERSON, JOHN, son of Thomas Henderson, a merchant in Dundee, was bapt. 17 Aug. 1726. [BN]

HENDERSON, JOHN, church member, 1781. [DCA.GD/EC/D10/1/2][S]

HENDERSON, JOHN, 4th son of Thomas Henderson nailer, born in New Gordon, Teviotdale, Roxburghshire, and his wife Elizabeth, dau. of James Taylor shepherd in Lauder, Berwickshire, born 24 Nov, bapt. 31 Dec. 1809. [E]

HENDERSON, MARY ANNE, dau. of Alexander Henderson and Sarah his wife, born 4 Oct., bapt. 13 Oct. 1816. [S]

HENDERSON, PETER, Excise officer, church member, 1810. [DCA.GD/EC/D10/1/2][S]

HENDERSON, THOMAS, a merchant in Dundee, 1727; church member and treasurer, 1743. [ECD] [DCA.GD/EC/DIO/2/1; 2/3]

HENDERSON, THOMAS, born 27 July, bapt. 13 Aug. 1826, 2nd son of the late George Henderson, a hatter, born in Stanhope, Durham, England, and his wife Ann, dau. of the late John Wishart a blacksmith in Dundee. [E]

HENDERSON, Mrs, church member, 1764. [DCA.GD/EC/DIO/2/1]

HENRY, BETSY, dau of Thomas Henry and Jane Goodlad, born 10 June 1805, bapt. 27 May 1813. [S]

HENRY, JEAN, pensioner, 1739. [DCA.GD/EC/DIO/2/1]

HENRY, JEAN, in Dundee, and William Jones, in Dundee, were married in the house of Rev. John Hetherton, Paton's Lane, Dundee, 21 Mar. 1833. [S]

HENRY, MARGARET, born 16 Oct., bapt. 1 Nov. 1829, 1st dau. of Samuel Henry, a canvas weaver, born in Lochcell, County Armagh, Ireland and his wife Elizabeth, dau. of William Day a weaver in Douglas, County Cork, Ireland. [E]

HEPBURN, MARY, dau. of James Hepburn and Janet Crighton, born 11 Mar. bapt 15 Aug. 1813. [S]

HETHERTON, JOHN, formerly in Arbroath, Angus, then in Morpeth, Northumberland, England, minister of the Qualified Episcopal Chapel, in Dundee, from 1809 until 1835. [Dundee Register, 1824][E] [DCA:GD/EC/D10/1/1-3]

HEWIT, Mrs, organist, 1816. [S][DCA.GD.EC.D10.1/2]

HIGH, Mrs, widow of John High, a pensioner, 1743. [DCA.GD/EC/D10/2/1]

HILL, ABRAM, 1784. [DCA.GD/EC/D10/2/2][E]

HILL, GEORGE, 1784. [DCA.GD/EC/D10/2/2][E]

HILL, JEAN, dau. of Alexander Hill, a cordiner in the Murraygait, Dundee, was bapt. 23 Sept 1726. [BN]

HILL, JOHN, a merchant in Dundee, 1727. [ECD]

HILL, ROBERT, in Dundee, 1727. [ECD]

HOLDEN, R. G., a vestryman, St Paul's, Dundee, in 1835. [DCA.GD.EC.10.1-3]

HOLLIDAY, CHARLES, born 2 Jan., bapt. 3 Feb. 1827, 4th son of John Holliday, a salmon fisher in Broughty Ferry, Angus, born in Annan, Dumfries-shire, and his wife Margaret, dau. of the late William Hackney, a merchant in Dundee. [E]

HOLLIDAY, JOHN, in West Ferry, and Margaret Hackney, both in Dundee were married 21 Feb. 1812. [E]

HOLLIDAY, JAMES, 1st son of John Holliday, a salmon fisher at West Ferry, Angus, born in Annan, Dumfries-shire, and his wife Margaret, dau. of William Hackney, a merchant in Dundee, born 13 Dec, bapt. 13 Jan. 1813. [E]

HOLLIDAY, GEORGE, born 12 July, bapt. 28 July 1829, 5th son of John Holliday, a salmon fisher late in Broughty Ferry, now in Dundee, born in Annan, Dumfries-shire, and his wife Margaret, dau. of the late William Hackney, merchant in Dundee. [E]

HOLLIDAY, HELEN, born 19 Jan, bapt. 20 Feb. 1821, 2nd dau of John Holliday, a salmon fisher late in Broughty Ferry, now in Dundee, born in Annan, Dumfries-shire, and his wife Margaret, dau. of the late William Hackney, merchant in Dundee. [E]

HOLLIDAY, JOHN THORNTON, born 5 Nov., bapt. 24 Nov. 1823, 3rd son of John Holliday, a salmon fisher late in Broughty Ferry, now in Dundee, born in Annan, Dumfries-shire, and his wife Margaret, dau. of the late William Hackney, merchant in Dundee. [E]

HOLLIDAY, MARGARET, born 3 July, bapt. 19 July 1818, dau. of John Holliday, a salmon fisher late in Broughty Ferry, now in Dundee, born in Annan, Dumfries-shire, and his wife Margaret, dau. of the late William Hackney, merchant in Dundee. [E]

HOLLIDAY, WILLIAM HACKNEY, 2nd son of John Holliday, a salmon fisher at West Ferry, Dundee, born in Annan, Dumfries-shire, and his wife Margaret, dau. of William Hackney merchant in Dundee, born 24 Mar. bapt. 13 Apr. 1814. [E]

HOLLINGER, JANE, born 16 Jan. bapt. 16 Feb. 1826, 2nd dau. of Joseph Hollinger, a weaver, born in Bellabay, County Monaghan, Ireland, and his wife Margaret, dau. of Thomas Haggart, a labourer in Callavy, County Antrim, Ireland. [E]

HOLLINGER, MARY, born 5 May, bapt. 15 June 1828, 2nd dau. of Joseph Hollinger, a weaver, born in Bellabay, County Monaghan Ireland, and his wife Margaret, dau. of Thomas Haggart, a laborer in Callavy, County Antrim, Ireland. [E]

HONEYMAN, CHRISTIAN, pensioner, 1739. [DCA.GD/EC/DIO/2/1]

HOOD, BELL, dau. of David Hood and Jane his wife, born 11 Feb. bapt. 27 May 1813. [S]

HOOD, BETSEY, dau. of David Hood and Jane his wife, born 10 Feb. 1809, bapt. 27 May 1813. [S]

HOOD, CHARLOTTE, dau. of Thomas Hood and Mary his wife, born 21 Jan. bapt. 31 Jan 1813. [S]

HOOD, MARY, dau. of David Hood and Jane his wife, born 16 Feb. 1811, bapt. 27 May 1813. [S]

HORN, ANN, 2nd dau of Alexander Horn brewer in Murraygait, Dundee, born in Dundee, and his wife Agnes Scott, dau. of John Scott, born in Ceres, Fife, was born 30 Dec. bapt. 31 Dec. 1808. [E]

HORN, PATRICK, stabler, church member, 1777. [DCA:GD/EC/D10/1/2][S]

HORSLEY, HENEAGE, minister of the Scottish Episcopal Chapel in Dundee, 1811.[S] [DCA.GD/EC/D10/1/2]; incumbent of St Paul's, Dundee, 1820s [DCA.GD.EC.D10.1/3]

HOW, JANET, dau. of David How and Elizabeth Bower, born 10 Jan., bap 28 July 1816. [S]

HOW, JOHN, son of John How and Elizabeth Langlands, born 15 June 1811, bapt. 26 Apr. 1812. [S]

HOW, JOHN, a member of the Scots Episcopal Chapel, Castle Street, Dundee, 1824. [DCA.GD.EC.D10.1/3]

HUGHES, DAVID REID, born 6 Dec., bapt. 31 Dec. 1826, 4th son of William Hughes, a gardener in Broughty Ferry, Angus, born in Dundee, and his wife Elizabeth, dau. of Robert Nicoll, a gardener at Woodlands, St Vigeans Angus. [E]

HUGHES, JAMES HALLIDAY, born 21 Oct., bapt. 24 Nov. 1823, 2nd son of William Hughes, a gardener in Broughty Ferry, Angus, born in Dundee, and his wife Elizabeth, dau. of Robert Nicoll, a gardener at Woodlands, St Vigeans Angus. [E]

HUGHES, WILLIAM, born 1 May., bapt. 5 June 1820, 1st son of William Hughes, a gardener in Broughty Ferry, Angus, born in Dundee, and his wife Elizabeth, dau. of Robert Nicoll, a gardener at Woodlands, St Vigeans Angus. [E]

HUNTER, ADAM, a bachelor in the parish of St George, Edinburgh, married Elizabeth Kirkcaldy, a spinster in Dundee, at Amelia Bank the residence of Mrs Kirkcaldy in Dundee, 3 Oct. 1820. [S]

HUNTER, ELIZABETH, a spinster of Rescobie, Angus, and Alexander Clayhills of Invergowrie, Perthshire, a bachelor in Dundee, were married in the house of Lieutenant General Hunter in Broughty Ferry, Angus, 10 Oct. 1826. [S]

HUNTER, ALEXANDER, of Balskellie, Angus, church member, 1758. [DCA.GD/EC/D10/2/2][E]

HUNTER, ALEXANDER CORK, son of Samuel Hunter and Barbara his wife born 20 Oct 1810, bapt 28 Mar. 1815. [S]

HUNTER, CATHERINE ERSKINE, dau. of Samuel Hunter and Barbara his wife born 15 Mar. bapt. 25 Mar. 1815. [S]

HUNTER, CHARLES, of Burnside, Angus, vestryman QEC, 1772; 1776, 1784. [DCA:GD/EC/D10/1/1] [DCA.GD/EC/D10/2/2][E]

HUNTER, DAVID, the younger, of Balskellie, Angus, vestryman of the QEC, 1768; 1776. [DCA:GD/EC/D10/1/1]

HUNTER, DAVID, of Blackness, Angus, vestryman of the QEC, 1772; 1776; 1784. [DCA:GD/EC/D10/1/1] [DCA.GD/EC/D10/2/2][E]

HUNTER, ELIZABETH CORK, dau. of Samuel Hunter and Barbara his wife, born 20 Oct. 1810, bapt. 28 Mar. 1815. [S]

HUNTER, ELIZABETH, a spinster of Rescobie, Angus, and Alexander Clayhills of Invergowrie, Perthshire, a bachelor in Dundee, were married in the house of Lieutenant General Hunter in Broughty Ferry, Angus, 10 Oct. 1826. [S]

HUNTER, JEMIMA, born 22 May, bapt. 26 June 1827, 1st dau. of James Hunter, a Private in the Rifle Brigade, born in Seaside, Perthshire, and his wife Jane, relict of the late James Stewart, and dau. of James MacDonald a labourer in Broughty Ferry, Angus. [E]

HUNTER, JOHN, son of Thomas Hunter and Mary his wife, born 22 Oct. bapt. 17 Nov. 1813. [S]

HUNTER, JOHN, a labourer in Dundee, widower, and Anne Littlejohn, a spinster in Dundee, were married in the vestry of St Paul's, Dundee, 28 Nov. 1824. [S]

HUNTER, Miss MARY, church member, 1746. [DCA.GD/EC/D10/2/1]

HUNTER, ROBERT, of the Customs House, member of the QEC, 1776; vestryman, 1781, 1784. [DCA:GD/EC/D10/1/1] [DCA.GD/EC/D10/2/2][E]

HUNTER, ROBERT, vestryman of the English Chapel, 1808. [E]

HUNTER, Captain, and his wife, members of the Scots Episcopal Chapel, Castle Street, Dundee, 1824. [DCA.GD.EC.D10.1/3]

HUSBAND, ALEXANDER, member of the QEC, 1776.
[DCA:GD/EC/D10/1/1]

HUSBANDS, MARIANNE, born 11 Feb. bapt. 25 Feb. 1821, 1st dau. of George Husbands, a Private in the 8th Royal Veteran Battalion, born in St Nicholas, Gloucester, England, and his wife Alice, dau. of Cornelius Dogherty, a labourer in Inniskilling, Ireland. [E]

HUTCHINSON, GEORGE, and Jean Chalmers, both in Dundee, married there 12 Apr. 1816. [E]

HUTCHINSON, HELEN, born 10 July, bapt. 23 July 1820, 3rd dau. of George Hutchinson, a carpenter's clerk born in Bervie, Kincardineshire, and his wife Jane, dau. of William Chalmers, a manufacturer in Liff, Angus. [E]

HUTCHISON, JAMES, a minister, from 1777 until 1779, St Mary's Chapel in Tally Street, Dundee, from 1779 until 1788.
[Dundee Directory, 1782, etc] [DCA.GD/EC/D10/1/2][S]

HUTCHINSON, HELEN, born 10 July, bapt. 23 July 1820, 3rd dau. of George Hutchinson, a carpenter's clerk born in Bervie, Kincardineshire, and his wife Jane, dau. of William Chalmers, a manufacturer in Liff, Angus. [E]

IDLEWIND, JANE WANNAN, 4th dau. of John Idlewind, a sugar baker, born in Reghan, Germany, and his wife Jane, dau. of Henry Shanks an invalid in Dundee, born 25 May, bapt. 30 May 1813. [E]

INGLIS, MARGARET, a spinster in Dundee, and William Stephen, writer, [lawyer] in Dundee, a bachelor, were married in the house of Mrs Inglis, Nethergait, Dundee, 9 Feb. 1835. [S]

INGRAM, CHRISTIAN, dau. of George Ingram and Jane Smith, born 15 June, bapt. 30 June 1811. [S]

INNES, CATHARINE, born 16 Nov., bapt. 22 Nov 1818, 3rd dau. of William Innes, a nailer, born in Dundee, and his wife Helen Anderson, dau. of James Anderson, labourer, born in Dundee. [E]

INNES, ELIZABETH, born 27 Dec. 1816, bapt. 1 Dec 1817, dau. of William Innes, a nailer, born in Dundee, and his wife Helen Anderson, dau. of James Anderson, labourer, born in Dundee. [E]

INNES, ROBERT, member of the QEC, 1776. [DCA:GD/EC/D10/1/1]

IRELAND, CHRISTIAN, dau. of John Ireland and Linda Calcoss (?), born 20 May, bapt. 26 May 1816. [S]

IRELAND, DAVID, stationer, and Elizabeth Jack, both in Dundee, were married 27 Sep. 1820. [E]

IRELAND, Mrs, a member of the Scots Episcopal Chapel, Castle Street, Dundee, 1824. [DCA.GD.EC.D10.1/3]

IRVINE, JAMES, minister of the Seagait Chapel, Dundee, from 1742 until 1743.

IVORY, JAMES, 1784. [DCA.GD/EC/D10/2/2][E]

JACK, ALEXANDER, member of the QEC, 1776. [DCA:GD/EC/D10/1/1

JACK, DAVID, a gardener, and Jean Smith, both in Dundee, were married 29 Nov.1824. [E]

JACK, ELIZABETH CATHERINE SKINNER, born 17 May, bapt. 21 May 1826, 1st dau. of Robert Jack, a Private of the 62nd Regiment of Foot, born in Montrose, Angus, and his wife Margaret, dau. of Robert Hill a skipper in Montrose. [E]

JACK, JAMES, in Dundee, 1727. [ECD]; church member, 1743. [DCA.GD/EC/DIO/2/1; 2/3] J

JAMIE, DAVID, a millwright, and Isabella Gilmour, both in Dundee, were married 27 Nov.1823. [E]

JAMIE, DAVID, born 17 Sept., bapt. 26 Sept. 1824, 1st son of David Jamie, a cabinetmaker, born in Montrose, Angus, and his wife Isabel, dau. of John Gilmour, a farmer in Strathmiglo, Fife. [E]

JAMIE, JOHN, born 21 Jan., bapt. 3 Feb. 1827, 1st son of David Jamie, a cabinetmaker, born in Montrose, Angus, and his wife Isabel, dau. of John Gilmour, a farmer in Strathmiglo, Fife. [E]

JAMIESON, DAVID, born 16 Mar., bapt. 28 Mar. 1817, son of Peter Jamieson, a travelling tinsmith, born in Dalmellington, Ayrshire, and his wife Mary, dau. of John Patrick, a weaver in Glasgow. [E]

JENERS, DAVID, son of George Jeners and Janet Burnet, born 27 Aug 1814, bapt. 11 June 1815. [S]

JENERS, JAMES, son of George Jeners and Elizabeth Urquhart, born 23 May, bapt. 26 June 1814. [S]

JENKINS, CLEMENTINA, born 22 Aug., bapt. 24 Aug.1828, dau. of Mary Jenkins, dau. of Robert Jenkins, a labourer in Kilmanoch, County Fermanagh, Ireland. [E]

JENKINS, JOHN, QEC vestryman, 1769; 1776. [DCA:GD/EC/D10/1/1]

JOBSON, GEORGE WILSON, born 1 Nov.1821, bapt. 5 Feb. 1822, 1st son of Christopher Jobson of West Haven, Angus, a Lieutenant of the Royal Navy, born in Eglingham, Northumberland, England, and his wife Elizabeth, dau. of George Wilson, wine merchant in Alnwick, Northumberland, and relict of John Ham of Alnwick. [E]

JOHNSON, SAMUEL, a bachelor in Islington, Middlesex, England, and Margaret Blakey, a spinster in Dundee, were married in St Paul's, Castle Street, Dundee, 2 Mar. 1830. [S]

JOHNSTON, ALEXANDER, of Baldovie, Angus, church member, 1777, 1781. [DCA:GD/EC/D10/1/2][S]

JOHNSTON, ANNABELLA, born 8 May, bapt. 26 May 1819, first dau. of Charles Johnston, a merchant born in Arbroath, Angus, and his wife Isabella, dau. of George Murray, late merchant in Dundee. [E]

JOHNSTON, CHARLES, a merchant, and Isabella Murray, both in Dundee, were married on 10 Aug. 1818. [E]

JOHNSTON, ELIZABETH, born 1 May, bapt. 5 May 1816, dau. of John Johnston a shoemaker in Lochee, born in Liff, Angus, and his wife Katherine Campbell dau. of John Campbell a labourer in Naboale, Argyll. [E]

JOHNSTONE, HENRY, a merchant in Bain's Square, Dundee, born 1771, died 25 Feb. 1809; vestryman of the QEC, 1803. [E] [DCA:GD/EC/D10/1/1]

JOHNSTON, HUGH, born 23 May, bapt. 31 May 1818, son of John Johnston, a shoemaker in Lochee, born in Liff, Angus, and his wife Katherine Campbell dau. of John Campbell a labourer in Naboale, Argyll. [E]

JOHNSTON, ISOBEL, dau. of James Johnston at the back of Powrie, Angus, was bapt. 13 Oct 1724. [BN]

JOHNSTON, ISOBEL, pensioner, 1740. [DCA.GD/EC/DIO/2/1]

JOHNSTON, ISABELLA, and George Bulloch, both of Dundee, were married in the house of Rev. John Hetherton, Paton's Lane, Dundee, 13 Dec. 1833. [S]

JOHNSTON, JAMES, of Clepington, Dundee, 1727. [ECD]

JOHNSTON, JEAN, dau. of Patrick Johnston, tenant in the Morrays [Murroes?], Angus, was bapt. 25 June 1726, godfather was John Fotheringham, brother german to the late George Fotheringham of Bandeen, with the wife of Dr Fotheringham and Mrs Beth Hay dau. of the late Sir John Hay of Moorie, Perthshire, as godmothers. [BN]

JOHNSTON, JOHN, son of James Johnston, a writer [lawyer] in Dundee, was bapt. 13 Aug. 1723. [BN]

JOHNSTON, MARY, born 1 Apr., bapt. 20 Apr. 1828, 2nd dau. of David Johnston, a shoemaker, born in Berwick-on-Tweed, Northumberland, England, and his wife Jane, dau. of Colin Mackenzie a shoemaker in Dundee. [E]

JOHNSTON, ROBERT MARSHALL, born 2 June, bapt. 5 Aug 1827, son of John Johnston a shoemaker in Lochee, born in Liff, Angus, and his wife Katherine Campbell dau. of John Campbell a labourer in Naboale, Argyll. [E]

JOHNSTON, WILLIAM, son of Peter Johnston in the Murraygait, Dundee, was bapt. 20 June 1724. [BN]

JOHNSTON, WILLIAM, and Ann Brown, both Dundee, were married at Reverend John Hetherton's house in Paton's Lane, Dundee, on 25 Oct. 1831. [S]

JOHNSTON, ..., church member, 1764. [DCA.GD/EC/DIO/2/1]

JOLLY, DAVID, joiner and turner in Dundee, born 1771, died 24 June 1809. [E]

JOLLY, DAVID, son of James Jolly and Hannah Pattullo, born 22 July, bapt. 1 Sept 1811. [S]

JOLLY, JAMES, church member, 1777. [DCA:GD/EC/D10/1/2][S]

JOLLY, JOHN, church member, 1811. [DCA:GD/EC/D10/1/1]

JONES, WILLIAM, in Dundee, and Jean Henry, in Dundee, were married in the house of Rev. John Hetherton, Paton's Lane, Dundee, 21 Mar. 1833. [S]

KAY, ISABEL, dau of Robert Kay and Anne Gray, born 21 May, bapt 19 July 1812. [S]

KAY, JOHN, born 9 May, bapt. 9 Aug. 1829, 3rd son of John Kay, a labourer, born in Gargonnoch, Stirlingshire, and his wife Sarah, dau. of John Holliday in Canterbury, Kent, England. [E]

KAY, ISABEL, dau. of Robert Kay and Anne Gray, born 21 May, bapt 19 July 1812. [S]

KEENS, JAMES HENRY, 2nd son of John Keens, Adjutant of the 25th Regiment of Foot, born in Isleworth, London, and his wife Martha, dau. of John Boyt in Starminster, Dorset, England, born 24 Feb. bapt. 6 April 1810. [E]

KEENS, THOMAS, son of John Keens, Sergeant of the 25th Regiment, born in Isleworth, Middlesex, England, and his wife Martha born in Stirminster, Dorset, England, dau. of John Boyt, born 24 Sept, bapt. 2 Oct. 1808. [E]

KEILLER, BARBARA, dau. of John Keiller and Betty his wife, born 16 Aug. bapt. 1 Sep 1817. [S]

KEILLER, ELLEN, dau. of John Keiller and Betty his wife, born 6 June bapt. 23 June 1816. [S]

KEITH, DAVID, a vestryman, St Paul's, Dundee, 1830. [DCA.GD.EC.D10.1-3]

KEITH, THOMAS, a vestryman, St Paul's, Dundee, 1830 [DCA.GD.EC.D10.1-3]

KILGOUR, CHARLES, born 30 Apr., bapt. 24 May 1825, 5th son of James Kilgour, a butcher born in Dundee, and his wife Elizabeth, dau. of George Mew, a mariner in Poole, Hampshire, England. [E]

KILGOUR, JANE WATT, born 28 Nov. 1820, bapt.1 Jan. 1820, 6th dau. of James Kilgour a butcher born in Dundee, and his wife Elizabeth, dau. of George Mew, a mariner in Poole, Hampshire, England. [E]

KILGOUR, JANET, born 3 Jan. 1817, bapt. 9 Feb 1817, dau. of James Kilgour a butcher born in Dundee, and his wife Elizabeth, dau. of George Mew, a mariner in Poole, Hampshire, England. [E]

KELLY, HAMILTON, 1st son of James Kelly, a Private in the Band of the 25th Regiment of Foot, born in St John's, Newcastle, Northumberland, England, and his wife Ann, dau. of John Robinson in Dundee, born 16 Sept. bapt. 25 Sept. 1809. [E]

KENNEDY, ALEXANDER, son of James Kennedy and Nancy his wife, born 16 Sept. bapt. 28 Jan. 1812. [S]

KENNEDY, CATHERINE, 5th dau of Peter Kennedy, a mariner, born in Forgan, Fife, and his wife Eleanor, dau of James Corrie weaver, born in Longforgan, Perthshire, born 20 May, bapt. 22 May 1809. [E]

KENNEDY, GEORGE, born 26 July, bapt. 22 Nov. 1825, 1st son of the late John Kennedy, gardener to the Marquis of Sutherland, born in Hull, Yorkshire, England, and his wife Ann, dau. of John Stewart a blacksmith in Norwich, Norfolk, England,"she was on her journey to her native place". [E]

KENNEDY, ISABELLA, 6th dau. of Peter Kennedy, a mariner, born in Forgan, Fife, and his wife Eleanor, dau. of James Corrie weaver, born in Longforgan, Perthshire, born 28 May, bapt. 1 June 1811. [E]

KENNEDY, JOHN, a bachelor in Dundee, married Lilias Phin, a spinster in Dundee, in her father's house in the Overgait, Dundee, 16 July 1827. [S]

KENNEDY, NEIL, son of John Kennedy and Margaret Smith, born 24 Jan., bapt. 20 Mar. 1816. [S]

KENNEDY, SOPHIA, 7th dau. of Peter Kennedy, a mariner, born in Forgan, Fife, and his wife Eleanor, dau. of James Corrie weaver, born in Longforgan, Perthshire, born 12 Aug, bapt. 14 Aug. 1813. [E]

KENNEDY, WILLIAM, 9th son of Peter Kennedy, a mariner, born in Forgan Fife, and his wife Eleanor, dau. of James Corrie weaver, born in Longforgan, Perthshire, born 11 June, bapt. 13 June 1815. [E]

KERR, ANNE HACKNEY, born 9 May, bapt. 12 June 1829, 3rd dau. of Christopher Kerr, writer and town clerk, born in Dundee, and his wife Jane, dau. of the late William Hackney a merchant in Dundee. [E]

KERR, ELIZABETH, born 21 Aug., bap. 17 Sep. 1829, 1st dau. of John Kerr, a writer, [lawyer], born in Dundee, and his wife Elizabeth, dau. of Patrick Bowie. [S]

KERR, GEORGE, a sailor, and Isabella Foulis, both of Dundee, were married on 16 Feb. 1812. [E]

KER, JAMES, in Dundee, 1727. [ECD]

KERR, JAMES, 1st son of William Kerr, a ships carpenter, born in Inverarity, Angus, and his wife Isabella, dau. of James Walls, a wright in Dundee, born 1 Mar. bapt. 9 Mar. 1811. [E]

KERR, JANE HACKNEY, born 11 Sep., bapt. 11 Oct. 1827, 3rd dau. of Christopher Kerr, writer and town clerk, born in Dundee, and his wife Jane, dau. of the late William Hackney a merchant in Dundee. [E]

KER, JOHN, a baker in Dundee, 1727. [ECD]; church member, 1743. [DCA.GD/EC/DIO/2/1; 2/3]

KERR, MARGARET HILL, and Thomas Nicholson, manager of the Railway Company, both in Dundee, were married in Mrs Kerr's house in Tay Street, Dundee, 20 Oct. 1834. [S]

KERR, MARGARET THORNTON, born 14 July, bapt. 12 Aug. 1826, 1st dau. of Christopher Kerr, writer and town clerk, born in Dundee, and his wife Jane, dau. of the late William Hackney a merchant in Dundee. [E]

KERIE, BESSIE, pensioner, 1740. [DCA.GD/EC/DIO/2/1]

KEY, ISABELLA, and David Nicoll, both of Dundee, were married in the vestry of St Paul's, Dundee, 20 Dec. 1833. [S]

KID, CLEMENTINA DUGANA, dau. of George Kid elder son of the laird of Craigie, Angus, was bapt. at Woodhill, Angus, 21 June 1722, godfather was the laird of Craigie her grandfather, while Madam Maitland and the lady Craigie her two grandmothers were godmothers. [BN]

KYD, DAVID, pensioner, 1739. [DCA.GD/EC/DIO/2/1]

KID, GEORGE, the younger of Craigie, in Dundee, 1727. [ECD]

KID, JAMES, of Craigie, in Dundee, 1727. [ECD]

KID, JOHN, son of Alexander Kid in the Hill of Mains, Angus, was bapt. 27 Sept. 1724. [BN]

KID, THOMAS, a merchant in Dundee, 1727. [ECD]

KILGOUR, ELIZA, 3rd dau. of James Kilgour, butcher in Murraygait, Dundee, born in Dundee, and his wife Elisabeth, dau. of George Mew, a mariner, born in Poole, Hampshire, England, born 9 Aug, bapt. 27 Aug 1809. [E]

KILGOUR, ISABELLA, 4th dau of James Kilgour, butcher in Murraygait, Dundee, born in Dundee, and his wife Elisabeth, dau. of George Mew, a mariner, born in Poole, Hampshire, England, born 22 Apr. bapt. 16 May 1813. [E]

KILGOUR, JAMES, 3rd son of James Kilgour, butcher in Murraygait, Dundee, born in Dundee, and his wife Elisabeth, dau of George Mew a mariner, born in Poole, Hampshire, England, born 8 Mar. bapt. 29 Apr. 1815. [E]

KININMOND, ALEXANDER, church member, 1743. [DCA.GD/EC/DIO/2/1; 2/3]

KININMOND, PATRICK, church member, 1758. [DCA.GD/EC/D10/2/2][E]

KININMOND, WILLIAM, church member, 1743. [DCA.GD/EC/DIO/2/1; 2/3]

KINLOCH, CECIL, dau. of Dr Kinloch in Dundee, was bapt. 20 June 1722. [BN]

KINLOCH, CHARLES, of Gourdie, Dundee, a church member, 1810. [DCA.GD/EC/D10/1/2][S]

KINLOCH, CHARLES, of the parish of Gourdie, Perthshire, residing in St Andrew's parish, Edinburgh, and Agnes Mylne, a spinster in Monifieth, Angus, residing in St George's parish, Edinburgh, were married at the house of Mrs Mackay, North Castle Street, Edinburgh, 25 July 1822. [S]

KINLOCH, JAMES, son of Dr John Kinloch in Dundee, was bapt. 1 Jan. 1726, godfathers were the laird of Kilrie and Dr David Fotheringham, while the wife of Dr Fotheringham was godmother. [BN]

KINLOCH, Sir JAMES, of that Ilk, in Dundee, 1727. [ECD], died in 1744.

KINLOCH, JAMES, the younger of that Ilk, in Dundee, 1727. [ECD]. A Jacobite in 1745, he died in Dundee on 5 February 1776. [Howff MI]

KINLOCH, JAMES, of Nevay, Angus, church member, 1743. [DCA.GD/EC/D10/2/3]

KINLOCH, JOHN, son of Dr John Kinloch in Dundee, was bapt. 24 June 1724, Patrick Crichton of Crunan and John Fotheringham, brother german to the late George Fotheringham of Bandeen were godfathers and the wife of Dr David Fotheringham was godmother. [BN]

KINLOCH, JOHN, son of the laird of Kilrie, was bapt. 15 Aug. 1724, godfathers were Dr John Kinloch and Dr David Fotheringham, with the wife of Dr John Kinloch being godmother. [BN]

KINLOCH, Dr JOHN, in Dundee, 1727. [ECD]

KINMOND, Mrs, member of the QEC, 1776. [DCA:GD/EC/D10/1/1]

KINNAIRD, ARTHUR FITZGERALD, son of Charles, Lord Kinnaird, and his wife Olivia born 8 July, bapt. 6 Aug. 1814. [S]

KINNAIRD, GRAHAM HAY ST VINCENT DE RUSSE, son of Charles, Lord Kinnaird, and his wife Olivia, bapt. 27 Nov. 1811. [S]

KINNAIRD, WILLIAM, born 29 June, bapt. 16 July 1826, 3rd son of George Kinnaird, a weaver, born in Leslie, Fife, and his wife Ann, dau. of Alexander Morris, a labourer in Kirkcaldy, Fife. [E]

KINNAIRD, Mrs, wife of Captain Kinnaird, church member, 1750. [DCA.GD/EC/DIO/2/1]

KINNAIRD, Lord, QEC committee, 1757. [DCA:GD/EC/D10/1/1] [DCA.GD/EC/D10/2/2][E]

KINNAIRD, Lady, church member, 1784. [DCA.GD/EC/D10/2/2][E]

KINNEAR, BETTY, dau. of James Kinnear and Betty Taylor, bapt. 16 Dec. 1811. [S]

KINNEAR, HUGH, pensioner, 1740; his relict, a pensioner, 1746. [DCA.GD/EC/DIO/2/1]

KIRKCALDY, ELIZABETH, a spinster in Dundee, married Adam Hunter a bachelor in the parish of St George, Edinburgh, at Amelia Bank the residence of Mrs Kirkcaldy in Dundee, 3 Oct. 1820. [S]

KNAPP, JANET JANE, 1st dau of Nicholson Knapp, master mariner of the Good Trow of Liverpool, and his wife Janet, dau. of John Anderson, farmer at Upper Claughan, Raffan, Banffshire, born 2 Sept. bapt. 14 Sept. 1811. [E]

KNIGHT, GEORGE, the younger, of Duncanstone, Angus, vestryman of the QEC, 1784. [DCA:GD/EC/D10/1/1]

KNIGHT, GEORGE, of Jordanstone, church member, 1810. [DCA.GD/EC/D10/1/2][S]

KNIGHT, Admiral JOHN, of Jordanstone, 1784. [DCA.GD/EC/D10/2/2][E]

KNIGHT, SARAH, born 21 Nov. bapt. 14 Dec.1828, 4th dau. of Alexander Knight, a travelling merchant, born in Airlie, Angus, and his wife Margaret, dau. of Robert Burgess, a nailer in Perth. [E]

KNIGHT, WILLIAM, 1739. [DCA.GD/EC/DIO/2/1]

KNOP, Captain NICHOLSON, born in Bremen, Germany, and Janet Anderson in Dundee, were married 25 Nov. 1810. [E]

KYLE, ROBERT, son of James Kyle and Ellen his wife, born 21 Aug, bapt. 19 Sept. 1813. [S]

LACKEY, ANN, 2nd dau. of John Lackey shoemaker, born in Maghargill, County Antrim, Ireland, and his wife Mary, dau. of Alexander Mackay, a labourer in Bellay, County Antrim, Ireland born 22 Apr. bapt. 1 May 1815. [E]

LAIRD, ANDREW, a merchant in Dundee, 1727. [ECD]; church member, 1750, 1758. [DCA.GD/EC/DIO/2/1] [DCA.GD/EC/D10/2/2][E] [a Jacobite in 1745]

LAIRD, ANDREW, a merchant, church member, 1777, 1781. [DCA:GD/EC/D10/1/2][S]

LAIRD, DAVID, member of the QEC, 1776. [DCA:GD/EC/D10/1/1]

LAIRD, Miss ISABELLA, a member of the Scots Episcopal Chapel, Castle Street, Dundee, 1824. [DCA.GD.EC.D10.1/3]

LAIRD, JAMES, a merchant in Dundee, 1727. [ECD]

LAIRD, JAMES, pensioner, 1739. [DCA.GD/EC/DIO/2/1]

LAIRD, WILLIAM (sic) ELIZABETH, a spinster in Strathmartin, Angus, and William Rowley Wynyard, a Lieutenant of the Royal Navy, a bachelor in Eccles, Berwickshire, were married in the house of David Laird in St Mary's, Angus, 11 Feb. 1830. [S]

LAMB, JAMES, member of the QEC, 1776. [DCA:GD/EC/D10/1/1]

LAMB, WILLIAM, 2nd son of Thomas Lamb mason in Chapelshade, Dundee, born in Kinclaven, Perthshire, and his wife Euphemia Reid, dau. of David Reid, a farmer, born in Kingoldrum, Angus, was born 17 Nov. bapt. 24 Dec. 1808. [E]

LAMBIE, Mrs, a church member, 1746. [DCA.GD/C/D10/2/1]

LAMMIE, ..., member of the QEC, 1776. [DCA:GD/EC/D10/1/1]

LAMONT, ANDREW, son of Donald Lamont, a Private in the 1st Battalion, of the Royal Regiment, and Leksie his wife, born 24 Dec. bapt. 31 Dec. 1815. [S]

LAMOND, JOHN, son of James Lamond and his wife Jane, born 24 Apl. bapt. 3 June 1816. [S]

LAMY, JOHN RAMSAY, vestryman of the QEC, 1757, 1777. [DCA:GD/EC/D10/1/1] [DCA.GD/EC/D10/2/2][E]

LAMY, JOHN, of Dunkennie, Angus, church member, 1784. [DCA.GD/EC/D10/2/2][E]

LAND, ..., church member, 1764. [DCA.GD/EC/DIO/2/1]

LANG, BETTY, dau. of Thomas Lang and his wife Barbara, born 7 June, bapt. 30 June 1811. [S]

LANGLANDS, HELEN, pensioner, 1739. [DCA.GD/EC/DIO/2/1]

LAURIE, DAVID, a member of the Scots Episcopal Chapel, Castle Street, Dundee, 1824. [DCA.GD.EC.D10.1/3]

LOUSON, ALEXANDER,

LAW, GEORGE, pensioner, 1739. [DCA.GD/EC/DIO/2/1]

LAW, JAMES, a merchant in Dundee, 1727. [ECD]

LAWSON, WILLIAM, son of James Lawson and Mary Marney, born 11 Nov, bapt 28 Dec 1814. [S]

LEECH, FRANCIS, member of the QEC, 1776. [DCA:GD/EC/D10/1/1]

LEITH, HECTOR, pensioner, 1739. [DCA.GD/EC/DIO/2/1]

LEISHMAN, JOHN, son of Arthur Leishman and Isabel his wife, born 15 May, bapt. 5 June 1815. [S]

LENIE, MARGARET, dau. of William Lenie and Ellen his wife, born 18 July, bapt. 25 July 1813. [S]

LESLIE, ROBERT, a bachelor in Dundee, and Mary Anderson, a spinster in Dundee, were married in the English Chapel, Nethergait, Dundee, 2 Aug. 1829. [S]

LEUCHARS, JAMES, a gardener, church member, 1764, 1777. [DCA:GD/EC/D10/1/2][S]

LIDDEL, ELIZABETH SPADDEN, dau. of John Liddel and Ellen his wife, born 18 Mar. bapt. 12 May 1816. [S]

LIDDELL, JAMES, pensioner, 1740. [DCA.GD/EC/DIO/2/1]

LIGHT, HENRY WILLIAM, 1st son of Alexander Whalley Light, Major of the 25TH Regiment of Foot, born in Palmcutta, East Indies, and his wife Jane Smart, dau. of John Smart, born in Frewitt, Northumberland, England, born 20 Oct. 1808 bapt. 28 Feb. 1809. [E]

LILLEY, ANNE, dau. of James Lilley and Mary his wife, born 17 Oct. bapt. 17 Nov. 1814. [S]

LILLEY, JAMES, bachelor in Inchture, Perthshire, and Mary Gunning, a spinster in Longforgan, Perthshire, were married on 31 Jan. 1814, witnessed by William Addison. [S]

LINDSAY, ALEXANDER, a baker in Liff, Angus, and Euphemia Proudfoot in Dundee, were married 31 May 1829. [E]

LINDSAY, ANN, born 29 Mar. bapt. 10 June 1828, 2nd dau. of Isaac Lindsay, a travelling tinsmith, born in Maghrafelt, County Londonderry, Ireland, and his wife Elizabeth, dau. of William Williamson a tinsmith in Stirling. [E]

LINDSAY, FRANCIS, born 29 Dec. bapt. 16 Jan. 1822, 2nd son of James Lindsay, a blacksmith, born in Montrose, Angus, and his wife Mary, dau. of Francis Wallace a merchant in Brechin, Angus. [E]

LINDSAY, JAMES CHARLES GOODCHILD, son of William Lindsay and Alison his wife, born 9 Jan. bapt. 8 Feb. 1812. [S]

LINDSAY, JAMES, born 24 Dec. 1819, bapt. 16 Jan. 1820, son of James Lindsay, a blacksmith, born in Montrose, Angus, and his wife Mary, dau. of Francis Wallace a merchant in Brechin, Angus. [E]

LINDSAY, JANE, dau. of John Lindsay and Jane Weighton, born 30 Apr. 1806 bapt. 20 Nov. 1814. [S]

LINDSAY, JEAN, dau. of Alexander Lindsay and Janet his wife, born 9 Sept. bapt. 18 Sept. 1814. [S]

LINDSAY, WILLIAM, pensioner, 1743. [DCA.GD/EC/D10/2/1]

LINDSAY, WILLIAM, member of the QEC, 1776. [DCA:GD/EC/D10/1/1]

LINDSAY, WILLIAM, a merchant, vestryman, 1802, 1810. [DCA.GD/EC/D10/1/2][S]

LINDSAY, WILLIAM, a vestryman, 1816/1817/1818/1820/1824. [S] [DCA.GD.EC.D10.1/2]

LINDSAY, ..., a sailor, and Margaret Ann Louis, were married on 25 July 1814. [E]

LINE, JOHN, a seaman, and Elizabeth Cook, both in Dundee, were married 30 Dec. 1827. [E]

LINN, JANET SANGSTER, born 30 Jan. bapt. 15 Feb. 1829, 3rd dau. of William Linn, a flax dresser, born in Moorchurch, Ayrshire, and his wife Elizabeth, dau. of James Macintosh, a chaise driver in Montrose, Angus. [E]

LITHGOW, ELIZABETH ANNE, dau. of James Lithgow and Isabell Adamson, born 17 May, bapt. 12 June 1814. [S]

LITTLEJOHN, ANNE, a spinster in Dundee, married John Hunter, a labourer in Dundee, widower, in the vestry of St Paul's, Dundee, 28 Nov. 1824. [S]

LIVINGSTON, ALEXANDER, son of Edward Livingston, a jeweller born in Edinburgh, and his wife Isabella, dau. of Thomas Speed, a shoemaker in Dundee, born 7 Aug. bapt. 13 Sept. 1812. [E]

LIVINGSTON, ANNE, 5th dau. of Edward Livingston, a jeweller, born in Edinburgh, and his wife Isabella, dau. of Thomas Speed, a shoemaker in Dundee, born 28 Oct. bapt. 10 Dec. 1809. [E]

LIVINGSTONE, MARJORY, born 15 Aug. 1832, bapt. 20 Aug. 1820, dau. of William Livingstone and his wife Elizabeth Campbell both from Glencraven, Argyll. [E]

LOUSON, ALEXANDER, son of John Louson and his wife Agnes, born 3 Aug. bapt. 11 Aug. 1816. [S]

LOW, ALEXANDER, son of Alexander Low and Janet Adam, born 10 Oct. 1805, bapt. 1 May 1815. [S]

LOWE, BARBARA, born 22 Feb. bapt. 9 Mar.1823, 1st dau. of Andrew Lowe, a rope-maker, born in Dundee, and his wife Jane, dau. of the late David Couty, a weaver in Dundee. [E]

LOW, CHRISTIAN, dau. of Abraham Low, a mason on the Hill of Dundee, was bapt. 6 June 1723. [BN]

LOWE, ELLEN, dau. of Andrew Lowe and Elizabth Rattray, was born on 1 May, bapt. on 3 June 1816. [S]

LOWE, EUPHEMIA, born 24 Mar. bapt. 13 Apr. 1821, 2nd dau. of Andrew Lowe, a rope-maker, born in Dundee, and his wife Jane, dau. of the late David Couty, a weaver in Dundee. [E]

LOWE, JANET, born 28 Feb. bapt. 13 Apr. 1826, 3rd dau. of Andrew Lowe, a rope-maker, born in Dundee, and his wife Jane, dau. of the late David Couty, a weaver in Dundee. [E]

LOW, KATHERINE, 1739. [DCA.GD/EC/DIO/2/1]

LOW, MARGARET, 1739. [DCA.GD/EC/DIO/2/1]

LOW, MARY ANNE, dau. of Andrew Low and Elizabeth Grimmond, born 24 June 1806, bapt. 14 Feb. 1813. [S]

LOWDON, ALEXANDER, a brewer, vestryman of the QEC, 1778. [DCA:GD/EC/D10/1/1]

LOWRIE, GEORGE, a bachelor in Dundee, and Ann Sparks, a spinster in Dundee, were married in the vestry of St Paul's, Castle Street, Dundee, 28 Oct. 1827. [S]

LOWSON, CIS, dau. of John Lowson and Agnes his wife, born 20 Apr, bapt. 7 May 1815. [S]

LOWSON, MARGARET WATT, dau. of John Lowson and Agnes his wife, born 9 Feb. bapt. 20 Feb. 1814. [S]

LUBEC, JEAN, dau. of Frederick Lubec and Margaret his wife, born 7 Nov. bapt. 10 Dec. 1813. [S]

LUNAN, ALEXANDER, and Isabel Ogilvy, both in Kinnettles, Angus, were married on 25 Oct. 1812. [E]

LUNDIE, JOHN, son of Thomas Lundie and his wife Susannah, bapt. 20 Feb. 1811. [S]

LUNDIE, MARY, dau. of Thomas Lundie and Susan Ken, born 24 Jan. bap. 26 Jan. 1817. [S]

LYAL, ELIZABETH, dau. of Hugh Lyal and his wife Margaret, born 7 Feb., bap. 9 Feb. 1817. [S]

LYALL, JESSIE DOUGLAS KEITH, dau. of William Lyall and Charlotte his wife, born 18 Feb. bapt. 19 Feb. 1815. [S]

LYALL, PETER, a baker, and Euphemia Wanless, both in Dundee, were married on 29 May 1809. [E]

LYALL, THOMAS, born 24 Sep. bapt. 24 Dec. 1826, 1st son of George Lyall, a carter, born in Dundee, and his wife Catharine, dau. of John Marshall a carter in Dundee. [E]

LYNCH, ELIZABETH, born 1 Dec. bapt. 20 Dec. 1829, 1st dau. of Matthew Lynch, a weaver, born in Mourane, County Down, Ireland, and his wife Sarah, dau. of William Ray a weaver in Mourane, County Down. [E]

LYNCH, ELIZABETH, a spinster in Dundee, and Andrew Cunningham, a widower in Dundee, were married in the house of Rev. H. Horsley, in Magdalene Yard, Perth Road, Dundee, 26 Feb. 1836. [S]

LYON, JAMES, in Dundee, 1727. [ECD]

LYON, PATRICK, burgh schoolmaster in Dundee, a Jacobite, was deposed in 1716. [NRS.CH2.103.8]

LYON, SUSANNA, dau. of James Lyon, merchant in the Nethergait, Dundee, was bapt. on 7 Feb. 1726, Provost Douglas of Forfar, Angus, was godfather while his wife and Mistress Malcolm were godmothers. [BN]

LYON, ..., wife of William Lyon, and her daughters Anne and Susan, church members, 1746. [DCA.GD/EC/D10/2/1]

LYON,........, church member, 1764. [DCA.GD/EC/DIO/2/1]

LYON, Miss, member QEC, 1776. [DCA:GD/EC/D10/1/1]

MCANDREW, SUSAN BOYD, born 6 Dec. 1824, bapt. 9 Jan. 1825, 1st dau. of Archibald McAndrew, born in Edinburgh, a travelling auctioneer, and his wife Mary, dau. of Thomas Wallace a labourer formerly a travelling merchant in Dundee. [E]

MACCABE, JOANNA, born 16 May, bapt. 8 June 1829, 1st dau. of Washington MacCabe, a weaver, in Ballybag, County Monaghan, Ireland, and his wife Mary, dau. of Dennis Sharkey a labourer in Glasgow. [E]

MCCASH, JAMES, vestryman, 1810/1816/1819. [S][DCA: GD/EC/D10.1/2]

MACCORMICK, ELLEN, dau. of Daniel MacCormick and Elizabeth Pearse, born 19 Nov. 1815, bapt. 18 Feb. 1816. [S]

MCCULLY, ROBERT, 1st son of Peter McCully, a Sergeant of the 21st Regiment of Foot, born in Paisley, Renfrewshire, and his wife Elizabeth, dau. of Matthew Burns, a Sergeant of the 21st Regiment of Foot, born 9 Dec. bapt 15 Dec. 1811. [E]

MCDONAGH, MARGARET, dau. of Kenneth McDonagh, a Private of the 79th Regiment, and Catherine his wife, born 28 Dec. bapt. 31 Dec. 1815. [S]

MCDONALD, ALEXANDER, in Dundee, 1727. [ECD]; pensioner, 1743. [DCA.GD/EC/D10/2/1]

MCDONALD, ALEXANDER, church member, 1764. [DCA.GD/EC/DIO/2/1]

MCDONALD, ALEXANDER, church member, 1781. [DCA.GD/EC/D10/1/2][S]

MACDONALD, ALEXANDER, born 19 Nov. bapt. 28 Nov. 1824, 4th son of Robert MacDonald, a labourer born in Inverness, and his wife Agnes, dau. of John Mackay, a weaver in Nigg, Easter Ross. [E]

MCDONALD, ELLEN, dau. of Peter McDonald and Ellen his wife, born 1 Sep. bapt. 22 Sep. 1816. [S]

MACDONALD, ISABELLA, born 9 Feb., bapt. 21 Feb. 1819, 1st dau. of Robert MacDonald, a labourer born in Inverness, and his wife Agnes, dau. of John Mackay, a weaver in Nigg, Easter Ross. [E]

MCDONALD, JOHN, church member, 1781. [DCA.GD/EC/D10/1/2][S]

MACDONALD, JOHN, organist of the QEC, 1784. [DCA:GD/EC/D10/1/1]

MACDONALD, JOHN, QEC church member, 1811. [DCA:GD/EC/D10/1/1]

MACDONALD, PETER, born 16 Jan. bapt. 18 Mar 1827, 5th son of Robert MacDonald, a labourer born in Inverness, and his wife Agnes, dau. of John Mackay, a weaver in Nigg, Easter Ross. [E]

MCDONALD, SARAH, born 20 Oct. bapt. 10 Nov. 1822, 2nd dau. of John Mackay a weaver in Nigg, Easter Ross. [E]

MACDONALD, WILLIAM, son of William MacDonald and Ellen Lindsay, born 24 Apr. bapt. 7 May 1815. [S]

MCDOUGALL, ELIZABETH GARD, born 16 Feb. bapt. 13 Feb. 1827, 2nd dau. of William MacDougall, Lieutenant in the Royal Navy, born in Dundee, and his wife Sally, dau. of Edward Snell, a farmer in Chorley, Devon, England. [E]

MCDOUGALL, MARTHA, born 21 May, bapt. 3 Aug. 1829, 3rd dau. of William MacDougall, Lieutenant in the Royal Navy, born in Dundee, and his wife Slly, dau. of Edward Snell, a farmer in Chorley, Devon, England. [E]

MCDOUGALL, MARY SPRY, born 26 May, bapt. 11 June 1824, 1st dau of William MacDougall, Lieutenant in the Royal Navy, born in Dundee, and his wife Sally, dau. of Edward Snell, a farmer in Chorley, Devon, England. [E]

MCDOUGALL, WILLIAM, a Lieutenant of the Royal Navy, married Sally Snell, both in Dundee, 12 May 1823. [E]

MCEWAN, Mrs, a member of the Scots Episcopal Chapel, Castle Street, Dundee, 1824. [DCA.GD.EC.D10.1/3]

MACFARLANE, JAMES, 3rd son of John MacFarlane, a Private of the 1st Battalion, of the 79th Regiment of Foot, born in Amulree, Perthshire, born 17 Feb. bapt. 8 Mar. 1811. [E]

MCGLASHAN, ALEXANDER, a merchant, QEC vestryman, manager, 1764, 1768, 1771. [DCA:GD/EC/D10/1/1; 2/2] [DCA.RD29.866][E]

MACGREGOR, ALEXANDER, 1st son of John MacGregor, a copper-smith, born in Montrose, Angus, and his wife Margaret, dau of Alexander Urquhart, a cork-cutter in Dundee, born 29 April, bapt 1 May 1811. [E]

MACGREGOR, CHARLES, bachelor in Perth, and Ann Mercer, spinster in Perth, were married on 6 July 1813 in Broughty Ferry, Angus, witnessed by ... Mercer. [S]

MACGREGOR, JANE URQUHART, born 10 Dec, bapt 14 Dec 1828, 3rd dau of John MacGregor, a copper-smith, born in Montrose, Angus, and his wife Margaret, dau of Alexander Urquhart, a cork-cutter in Dundee. [E]

MACGREGOR, JOHN, son of John MacGregor and Elizabeth Miller, born 24 Oct, bapt 22 Nov 1812. [S]

MCGREGOR, JOHN, born 21 May, bapt 25 May 1817, of John MacGregor, a copper-smith, born in Montrose, Angus, and his wife Margaret, dau of Alexander Urquhart, a cork-cutter in Dundee. [E]

MACGREGOR, MARGARET KER, born 1 May, bapt 9 May 1819, 1st dau of John MacGregor, a copper-smith, born in Montrose, Angus, and his wife Margaret, dau of Alexander Urquhart, a cork-cutter in Dundee. [E]

MCHARDIE, ANN, born 18 Apr., bap. 28 Apr. 1822, 2nd dau. of James McHardie, a joiner, born in Mar, Aberdeenshire, and his wife Janet, dau. of Peter Hay, a porter in Dundee. [E]

MCHARDIE, JAMES, and Charlotte Sturrock, both in Dundee, were married 19 Mar.1826. [E]

MCHARDIE, MARY, born 11 July, bap. 19 July 1829, 1st dau. of James McHardie, a wright, born in Braemar, Aberdeenshire, and his wife Charlotte, dau. of David Sturrock a baker in Dundee. [E]

MACINTOSH, AGNES, dau of John MacIntosh and Janet Gibson, born 26 June, bapt 1 Aug 1811. [S]

MACINTOSH, GILBERT, son of Duncan MacIntosh and his wife Margaret, born 27 Jan., bap. 4 Feb. 1816. [S]

MACINTYRE, JANE, dau of William MacIntyre and Barbara his wife, born 3 Mar, bapt 9 May 1813. [S]

MACINTIRE, JOHN, 3rd son of Peter MacIntire, a mariner of the Royal Navy, born in Haddington, East Lothian, and his wife Isabel, dau of James Nichol, a labourer in Dundee, born 2 Sept, bapt 10 Oct 1809. [E]

MACINTYRE, MARGARET, dau of Peter MacIntyre and Isabel his wife, born 31 Mar, bapt 22 Aug 1814. [S]

MACINTYRE, WILLIAM, and his wife, members of the Scots Episcopal Chapel, Castle Street, Dundee, 1824. [DCA.GD.EC.D10.1/3]

MACKAY, ANNE, dau. of William Mackay and Margaret Ferrier, born 11 Aug. 1815, bapt. 16 June 1816. [S]

MACKAY, BEL, dau. of Gordon Mackay and Margaret his wife, born 22 Mar. bapt. 7 Apr. 1816. [S]

MACKAY, JOHN, son of George Mackay and Barbara his wife, born 28 Apl., bapt. 12 May 1816. [S]

MACKAY, THOMAS, 2ND son of John Mackay, a labourer, born in Winchester, Hampshire, England, and his wife Mary, dau. of Thomas Nash, a gardener in Romsey, Hampshire, England, born 12 Mar. bapt. 18 Mar. 1810. [E]

MACKENZIE, ALEXANDER, 1st son of James MacKenzie, a porter, born in Blair Atholl, Perthshire, and his wife Margaret, dau. of John Addison, mariner in Dundee, born 25 Jan. bapt. 28 Jan. 1810. [E]

MACKENZIE, ANNE, dau. of Daniel Mackenzie and Anne his wife, born 5 Apr. bapt. 15 Apr. 1812. [S]

MCKENZIE, ANN, a spinster in Dundee, and Daniel MacLachlan, an assistant surgeon of the 79th Highlanders, were married in the house of Mrs MacKenzie, Annfield, near Dundee, 23 July 1834. [S]

MCKENZIE, CHARLES, born 25 May, bapt. 4 June 1826, 1st son of James Mackenzie, a wright, born in Braemar, Aberdeenshire, and his wife Charlotte, dau. of David Sturrock a baker in Dundee. [E]

MCKENZIE, DAVID, a gunsmith in Dundee, 1727. [ECD]

MACKENZIE, D., a member of the Scots Episcopal Chapel, Castle Street, Dundee, 1824. [DCA.GD.EC.D10.1/3]

MACKENZIE, ELIZABETH, dau. of Daniel Mackenzie and Anne his wife, born 31 Aug, bapt. 14 Sept. 1814. [S]

MACKENZIE, JANE, 1st dau. of James MacKenzie, a porter, born in Blair Atholl, Perthshire, and his wife Margaret, dau. of John Addison, a mariner in Dundee, born 6 Aug. bapt. 11 Aug. 1811. [E]

MACKENZIE, PETER, son of Peter MacKenzie and Mary Sinclair, born 16 Jan. bapt. 6 Feb. 1815. [S]

MACKENZIE, ROBERT, 2nd son of James MacKenzie, a porter, born in Blair Atholl, Perthshire, and his wife Margaret, dau. of John Addison a mariner in Dundee, born 1 Nov. bapt. 7 Nov. 1813. [E]

MCKENZIE, Mr, church member, 1764. [DCA.GD/EC/DIO/2/1]

MCKENZIE, Mrs, member QEC, 1776. [DCA:GD/EC/D10/1/1]

MACLACHLAN, DANIEL, an assistant surgeon of the 79th Highlanders, a bachelor, and Ann MacKenzie, a spinster in Dundee, were married in the house of Mrs MacKenzie, Annfield, near Dundee, 23 July 1834. [S]

MCLACHLAN, MARGARET, dau. of Daniel MacLachlan and Elizabeth his wife, born 30 June, bapt. 20 July 1816. [S]

MACLAREN, WILLIAM, son of John MacLaren and Susan Paterson, born 8 Mar. bapt. 18 Oct. 1812. [S]

MACLEOD, WALTER, 5th son of Daniel MacLeod hatter, born in Nairn, Nairnshire, and his wife Margery, dau. of Walter Ross, a spoonmaker in Perth, born 6 Nov. bapt. 11 Nov. 1810. [E]

MCMILLAN, ROBERT, born 25 Sep. bapt. 4 Oct. 1829, 1st son of Robert MacMillan, born in Bally, County Antrim, Ireland, and his wife Janet dau. of James Fell, a labourer in Dundee. [E]

MACNAB, ANN, 1st dau of John MacNab, a nailer, born in Dunkeld, Perthshire, and his wife Ann, dau. of Thomas MacNab, a labourer in Dundee, born 27 May bapt. 1 June 1811. [E]

MACNAB, DANIEL, 1st son of Daniel Macnab, a mariner in the Royal Navy, born in Edinburgh, and his wife Margaret, dau. of James Johnston, a tailor, born in Edinburgh, born 13 Dec. 1808, bapt. 15 Jan. 1809. [E]

MACNAB, JAMES, a bachelor in Dundee, and Margaret Mitchell, a spinster in Dundee, were married in the vestry of St Paul's, Castle Street, Dundee, 27 May 1828.

MCNAB, JOHN, QEC church member, 1811. [DCA:GD/EC/D10/1/1]

MACNAIR, ANDREW GALLOWAY, 3rd son of David MacNair, a pensioner of the Royal Scots Regiment, born in Kinross, Kinross-shire, and his wife Margaret, dau. of Alexander Crichton, a weaver in Arbroath, Angus, born 16 May, bapt. 18 May 1812. [E]

MACNAIR, ELIZABETH, 2nd dau of David MacNair, a pensioner of the Royal Scots Regiment, born in Kinross, and his wife Margaret, dau. of Alexander Crichton, a weaver in Arbroath, born 1 Apr. bapt. 12 Apr. 1810. [E]

MACNAIR, MARGARET, 3rd dau of David MacNair, a pensioner of the Royal Scots Regiment, born in Kinross, and his wife Margaret, dau. of Alexander Crichton, a weaver in Arbroath, born 22 Jan, bapt. 29 Jan. 1815. [E]

MACNAIR, WILLIAM, a soldier of the 72nd Regiment, and Elizabeth Kay, both in Dundee, were married 29 Jan. 1826. [E]

MACNIEL, ELIZABETH, dau. of William MacNiel and Margaret Phelp, born 16 Dec. 1814, bapt. 1 Jan. 1815. [S]

MACONNACHIE, ELIZABETH, born 4 Feb. bapt. 9 Feb.1829, 1st dau. of Henry MacOnnichie, a chimney sweeper, born in County Armagh, Ireland, and his wife Elizabeth, dau. of John Scott a tinsmith in Perth. [E]

MACORMICK, ELLEN, dau. of Daniel MacOrmick and Elizabeth Pearce, born 10 Nov. 1815, bapt. 18 Feb. 1816. [S]

MCPHERSON, ANNE, dau. of John MacPherson and Sally his wife, born 4 Oct. bapt. 9 Oct. 1811. [S]

MACPHERSON, JAMES, son of Saunders MacPherson and Jane his wife, born 25 Mar. bapt. 9 Apr. 1815. [S]

MCPHERSON, JAMES PETER, son of Peter McPherson and Elizabeth his wife, born 14 Nov., bapt. 1 Dec. 1816. [S]

MACQUEEN, JAMES, son of Frank MacQueen and Mary Cooke, born 21 July, bapt. 15 Aug. 1813. [S]

MACQUEEN, JAMES, son of Frank MacQueen and Margaret Preston, born 6 Nov. bapt. 28 Nov. 1813. [S]

MACRAE, CATHERINE, dau. of Daniel MacRae and Jane his wife, born 21 Mar. bapt. 13 Aug. 1815. [S]

MACRITCHIE, ANNE, dau of William MacRitchie and Anne Rattray, born 1807, bapt. 7 Nov. 1811. [S]

MACWHATTIE, JAMES, son of David MacWhattie and Ellen his wife, born 12 Mar. bapt. 26 Apr. 1815. [S]

MCWILLIAM, JANE, born 12 Mar., bapt. 9 Apl. 1819, 1st dau. of John McWilliam, a stocking weaver, born in Glasgow, and Jane, dau. of Matthew Bailey a labourer in Tranent, East Lothian. [E]

MADISON, THOMAS, son of Robert Madison at the Miln of Mains, Dundee, was bapt. 18 July 1726. [BN]

MAIDEN, ALEXANDER, pensioner, 1746. [DCA.GD/EC/D10/2/1]

MAIDEN, JAMES JOHN, son of John Maiden, weaver in Cottarton of Craigie, Angus, was bapt. 7 Oct. 1726. [BN]

MAITLAND, JOHN, an Excise officer, QEC vestryman 1768. [DCA:GD/EC/D10/1/1]

MALCOLM, JAMES, son of James Malcolm and Margaret Small, born 19 Sept. bapt. 2 Oct. 1814. [S]

MALLART, THOMAS CHARLES, 1st son of Joseph Mallart, a Private of the 70th Regiment of Foot, born in Killala, County Cavan, Ireland, and his wife Margaret, dau. of John Gillilands, a weaver in Lurgan, County Meath, Ireland, born 26 Dec. bapt. 12 Jan. 1814. [E]

MANDERSTON, JAMES, a merchant and dyer in Dundee, 1727. [ECD]

MANKIN, SARAH, wife of Patrick Miller, clerk to the Pleasance Brewery, in Upper Pleasance, Dundee, born 1776, died 17 June 1809. [E]

MANN, CATHERINE YOUNG, dau. of Peter Mann and Elizabeth Robertson, born 26 May, bapt. 12 June 1814. [S]

MANN, HENRY, son of Robert Mann and Elizabeth Birnie, born 9 Oct. bapt. 25 Oct. 1812. [S]

MANN, MARY ANN, dau. of John Mann and his wife Anne, born 28 June, bapt. 21 July 1816. [S]

MANNEA, ROBERT, son of William Mannea and Nelly his wife, born 28 Dec. 1811, bapt. 1 Jan. 1812. [S]

MARSHALL, AGNES, a spinster in Ferryport-on-Craig, Fife was married at the house of Mrs Addison, High Street, Dundee, 31 Dec. 1820. [S]

MARSHAL, ALEXANDER, son of Robert Marshal and Isabella his wife, born 5 Jan. bapt. 20 Jan. 1812. [S]

MARSHALL, ANN, born 1 Feb. bapt. 2 Feb. 1829, 1st dau. of Peter Marshall, a tinsmith, born in Dunfermline, Fife, and his wife Elizabeth, dau. of Daniel Marshall, a coppersmith in Dunfermline. [E]

MARSHAL, DAVID, son of Andrew Marshal and Margaret his wife, born 6 Nov. bapt. 6 Dec. 1812. [S]

MARSHAL, DAVID, son of James Marshal and Jane his wife, born 3 Sept. bapt. 11 Sept. 1814. [S]

MARSHAL, ISABELLA, 5th dau. of William Marshal, a Sergeant of the 91st Regiment of Foot, born in Perth, and his wife Jane, dau. of Felix Nicholson, a maltmaker in Monnymoor, Hartrag, Londonderry, Ireland, born 29 Apr. bapt. 16 May 1813. [E]

MARSHALL, JAMES, a shoemaker in Dundee, 1743. [ECD]

MARSHALL, JANET, church member, 1764. [DCA.GD/EC/DIO/2/1]

MARSHALL, JOHN, church member, 1764. [DCA.GD/EC/DIO/2/1]

MARSHAL, PETER, son of Andrew Marshal and Margaret his wife, born 6 Dec. bapt. 15 Dec. 1816. [S]

MARSHALL, THOMAS, born 20 Feb. bapt. 21 Mar. 1828, 4th son of Robert Marshall, a weaver, born in Glamis, Angus, and his wife Jane, dau. of David Smith, a weaver in Dundee. [E]

MARSHALL, WILLIAM, merchant, and Catharine Middleton, both in Dundee, were married 10 Mar.1823. [E]

MARTIN, ABIGAIL, born 27 Feb. bapt. 7 Mar. 1824, 3rd dau. of Hugh Martin, a labourer, former Private in the 8th Royal Veteran Battalion, born in Ballingins, County Antrim, Ireland, and his wife Abigail, dau. of Dennis MacReady, a labourer in Ballyshanney, County Donegal, Ireland. [E]

MARTIN, ANN, dau. of John Martin travelling chapman, born in Carlisle Cumberland, England, and his wife Mary, dau. of William Coyles, a butcher in Ballycastle, County Antrim, Ireland, born 29 Apr. bapt. 24 May 1813. [E]

MARTIN ANN, born 1 Jan. bapt. 6 Jan. 1823, 3rd dau. of Hugh Martin, a labourer, former Private in the 8th Royal Veteran Battalion, born in Ballingins, County Antrim, Ireland, and his wife Abigail, dau. of Dennis MacReady, a labourer in Ballyshanney, County Donegal,

Ireland. [E]

MARTIN, CATHERINE, dau. of William Martin and Jane Fenton, born 19 Nov, 1816, bap. 19 Jan. 1817. [S]

MARTIN, CATHERINE, born 27 July, bap. 15 Aug. 1819, fourth dau. of Robert Martin, a labourer born in Liff, Angus, and his wife Elizabeth, dau. of James Langlands a tailor in Dundee. [E]

MARTIN, HUGH, born 13 Oct, bapt. 21 Oct. 1829, 3rd son of Hugh Martin, a labourer, former Private in the 8th Royal Veteran Battalion, born in Ballingins, County Antrim, Ireland, and his wife Abigail, dau. of Dennis MacReady, a labourer in Ballyshanney, County Donegal, Ireland. [E]

MARTIN, JEAN, dau. of William Martin in Logie, Dundee, was bapt. 3 July 1723. [BN]

MARTIN, JOHN, a brewer in Dundee, 1727. [ECD]

MARTIN, JOHN, a sailor, and Amelia Nucator, both in Dundee, were married 31 Oct. 1823. [E]

MARTIN MARY, born 16 Oct, bapt. 29 Oct. 1820, 1st dau of Hugh Martin, a labourer, former Private in the 8th Royal Veteran Battalion, born in Ballingins, County Antrim, Ireland, and his wife Abigail, dau. of Dennis MacReady, a labourer in Ballyshanney, County Donegal, Ireland. [E]

MARTIN Mary, born 24 Jan, bapt. 24 Jan. 1826, 2nd dau. of Hugh Martin, a labourer, former Private in the 8th Royal Veteran Battalion, born in Ballingins, County Antrim, Ireland, and his wife Abigail, dau. of Dennis MacReady, a labourer in Ballyshanney, County Donegal, Ireland. [E]

MARTIN MARY, born 25 Feb, bapt. 2 Mar. 1828, 5th dau. of Hugh Martin, a labourer, former Private in the 8th Royal Veteran Battalion, born in Ballingins, County Antrim, Ireland, and his wife Abigail, dau. of Dennis MacReady, a labourer in Ballyshanney, County Donegal, Ireland. [E]

MARTIN, WILLIAM, son of James Martin and Mary Smart, born 10 Jan, bapt. 20 Dec 1812. [S]

MASON, WILLIAM, a labourer in Dundee, a widower, and Janet Ferguson, a spinster in Dundee, were married in St Paul's Chapel, Dundee, 5 Sep. 1824. [S]

MASTERTON, JANE, 1st dau. of William Masterton, a mariner, born in Forfar, Angus, and his wife Elizabeth, dau of John Elder, a porter in Dundee, born 4 Nov, bapt. 7 Nov. 1813. [E]

MATHESON, ROBERT, a wright in Dundee, 1727. [ECD]

MATHEW, DAVID, a dyer in Murraygait, Dundee, 1727. [ECD]

MATTHEW, JANE, born 29 July, bapt. 15 Aug. 1819, first dau. of James Matthew, a weaver and starcher, born in Dundee, and his wife Jane, dau of William Peter, a stone-mason in Dundee. [E]

MATHEW, JANET, dau. of David Mathew,a dyer in the Murraygait, Dundee, was bapt. 25 May 1724. [BN]

MATHEW, JOHN, a wright, church member, 1777, 1781. [DCA:GD/EC/D10/1/2][S]

MATTHEW, JOHN, a merchant, vestryman, 1802, 1810. [DCA.GD/EC/D10/1/2][S]

MATHEW, JOHN, and his wife, members of the Scots Episcopal Chapel, Castle Street, Dundee, 1824. [DCA.GD.EC.D10.1/3]

MATHEW, PATRICK, son of David Mathew, a dyer in the Murraygait, Dundee, was bapt. 14 Aug. 1722. [BN]

MAURICE, JEAN, dau. of William Maurice, a weaver in the Seagait, Dundee, was bapt. 25 Feb. 1723. [BN]

MAWER, JOHN, a dyer in Dundee, 1727. [ECD]; church member, 1743. [DCA.GD/EC/DIO/2/1; 2/3]

MAWER, ROBERT, in Dundee, and Elizabeth Palmer, in Panbride, Angus, marriage banns, 10 Sept. 1815. [E]

MAWER, Mrs, a member of the Scots Episcopal Chapel, Castle Street, Dundee, 1824. [DCA.GD.EC.D10.1/3]

MAXWELL, PATRICK, 1784. [DCA.GD/EC/D10/2/2][E]

MAY, BETTY ANNE, dau. of George May and Anne his wife, born 29 June, bapt. 12 July 1812. [S]

MAY, THOMAS PITCAIRN, son of George May and Anne his wife, born 9 Oct, bapt. 16 Oct. 1814. [S]

MEAL, ROBERT, in Dundee, 1727. [ECD]

MEFFAN, ELIZABETH, 1st dau. of John Meffan weaver, born in Dundee, and his wife Isabell, dau. of William Banks, a weaver in Dundee, born 8 Jan, bapt. 23 Jan. 1815. [E]

MENIE, MARGARET, dau. of William Menie and Ellen his wife, born 18 July bapt. 25 July 1813. [S]

MENZIES, CATHARINE, born 10 Dec. bapt. 31 Dec. 1820, third dau. of Duncan Menzies, a labourer born in Breadalbane, Perthshire, and his wife Margaret, dau. of Donald MacLaggan a farmer in Breadalbane. [E]

MENZIES, or MANZIE, DAVID, wright, church member, 1777, 1781. [DCA:GD/EC/D10/1/2][S]

MENZIES, DAVID, a pensioner aged 74 in 1818. [S][DCA.GD.EC.D10.1/2]

MENZIES, JAMES, of Woodend, vestryman of the QEC, 1757; 1764. [DCA:GD/EC/D10/1/1]

MENZIES, JAMES, of Menzieshill, Angus, QEC vestryman, 1768. [DCA:GD/EC/D10/1/1] [DCA.GD/EC/D10/2/2][E]

MENZIES, JOHN, church member, 1784. [DCA.GD/EC/D10/2/2][E]

MENZIES, the Misses, church members,1810. [DCA.GD/EC/D10/1/2][S]

MENZIES, Miss, a member of the Scots Episcopal Chapel, Castle Street, Dundee, 1824. [DCA.GD.EC.D10.1/3]

MENZIES, Miss MARY, a member of the Scots Episcopal Chapel, Castle Street, Dundee 1824/1828. [DCA.GD.EC.D10.1/3]

MERCER,....., a member of the Scots Episcopal Chapel, Castle Street, Dundee, 1824. [DCA.GD.EC.D10.1/3]

METCALFE, CAROLINE MARIA, 3rd dau. of Captain Thomas Levett Metcalfe of the 2nd Battalion, 79th Regiment of Foot, born in Queen Anne Street East, Chapelry of Portland Place, London, and his wife Jane Hamilton Casy, dau. of Micah Casy of Donagh Carn, Count Donegal, Ireland, born 5 Aug. bapt. 24 Aug. 1810. [E]

MICKLEROY, ANN, born 9 May, bapt. 5 July 1829, 1st dau. of Edward Mickleroy, a weaver, born in Ballimony, County Londonderry, Ireland, and his wife Sibill, dau. of Thomas MacAnless a weaver in Dundee. [E]

MIDDLETON, JAMES, QEC church member, 1811. [DCA:GD/EC/D10/1/1]

MIDDLETON, JAMES, son of David Middleton and Elizabeth his wife, born 28 Mar, bapt. 20 Apr. 1813. [S]

MIDDLETON, JANE, dau. of Robert Middleton and Elizabeth Henry, born 11 May, bapt. 12 June 1814. [S]

MIDDLETON, JANET, dau. of Robert Middleton and Elizabeth Henry, born 26 Sept. bapt. 29 Sept. 1811. [S]

MILL, CATHERINE, a spinster in Leuchars, Fife, married William Smith, a labourer in Leuchars, a bachelor, at the house of Mrs Addison, High Street, Dundee, 9 May 1819. [S]

MILL, ELSPET, a pensioner aged 60-70 in 1818. [S] [DARC.GD.EC.D10.1/2]

MILL, ROBERT, farmer, church member, 1777. [DCA.GD/EC/D10/1/2][S]

MILL, Mrs, member of the QEC, 1776. [DCA:GD/EC/D10/1/1]

MILLER, CHRISTIAN, dau. of William Miller in Whitfield, Angus, bapt. 12 Jan. 1723. [BN]

MILLER, DANIEL, son of Daniel Miller and Margaret Culbert, born 1 May. bapt. 29 May 1814. [S]

MILLER, DAVID, son of James Miller in Logie, Dundee, bapt. 18 July 1722. [BN]

MILLAR, Mrs DAVID, of Ballumbie, Angus, church members, 1810. [DCA.GD/EC/D10/1/2][S]

MILLER, Miss E., a member of the Scots Episcopal Chapel, Castle Street, Dundee, 1824. [DCA.GD.EC.D10.1/3]

MILLAR, ELIZABETH, 2nd dau. of Patrick Millar, clerk to the Pleasance Brewery, Dundee, born in Tealing, Angus, and his wife Sarah, dau. of Thomas Rankin, a coal-broker in Whitechapel Street, London, born 14 Jan, bapt. 1 Feb. 1810. [E]

MILLER, ELIZABETH, a spinster in Dundee, and David Mitchell, a bachelor in Dundee, were married in her father's house in High Street, Dundee, on 14 Sep. 1828. [S]

MILLER, HELEN, a member of the Scots Episcopal Chapel, Castle Street, Dundee, 1824. [DCA.GD.EC.D10.1/3]

MILLER, JAMES, vestryman, 1802. [DCA.GD/EC/D10/1/2][S]

MILLER, MARGARET, dau. of James Miller in Cottarton of Dudhope, Dundee, was bapt. 27 Jan. 1726. [BN]

MILLER, MARGARET, dau. of Thomas Miller and Margaret Buist, born 14 June, bapt. 30 July 1815. [S]

MILLER, MARGARET, dau. of James Miller and his wife Anne, born 23 Aug., bapt. 1 Sep. 1816. [S]

MILLER, MARY, a member of the Scots Episcopal Chapel, Castle Street, Dundee, 1824. [DCA.GD.EC.D10.1/3]

MILLER, PATRICK, church member, 1811. [DCA:GD/EC/D10/1/1]

MILLER, THOMAS, in Dundee, 1727. [ECD]

MILLER, WILLIAM, in Dundee, 1727. [ECD]

MILLAR, WILLIAM, organist of the QEC, 1776. [DCA:GD/EC/D10/1/1] [DCA.GD/EC/D10/2/2][E]

MILLER, WILLIAM, a jeweller, and Elizabeth Fitchett, both in Dundee, were married 22 Nov. 1816. [E]

MILLER, ..., and his wife, members of the Scots Episcopal Chapel, Castle Street, Dundee, 1824. [DCA.GD.EC.D10.1/3]

MILLAR, Mrs, among the 'poor of Mr Hetherton's congregation in Dundee, 1830'. [DCA.GD.EC.D10.1/3]

MILNE, ANNE, dau. of William Milne and Margaret his wife, born 24 Mar. bapt. 21 Aug. 1814. [S]

MILNE, DAVID, born 23 Feb., bapt. 1 Mar. 1818, son of David Milne, a chapman, born in Glamis, Angus, and his wife Janet, dau. of George Methven, a labourer in Cupar, Fife. [E]

MILNE, ISABELL, a spinster in Dundee, and John Anderson, a bachelor in Dundee, were married in the house of Rev. Heneage Horsley, Magdalene Yard, Dundee, 2 Apl. 1834. [S]

MILN, MARGARET, 1st dau of David Miln, a chapman, born in Glamis, Angus, and his wife Janet, dau. of George Methven, a labourer in Cupar, Fife, born 18 Apr, bapt. 25 Apr. 1813. [E]

MILN, THOMAS, of Milnfield, Perthshire, QEC committee, 1757; vestryman 1764, 1768; 1776, 1784. [DCA:GD/EC/D10/1/1] [DCA.GD/EC/D10/2/2][E]

MILNE, Mrs, a member of the Scots Episcopal Chapel, Castle Street, Dundee, 1824. [DCA.GD.EC.D10.1/3]

MITCHELL, ALEXANDER, church member, 1743.
[DCA.GD/EC/DIO/2/1; 2/3]

MITCHELL, ALEXANDER, gardener, church member, 1777.
[DCA.GD/EC/D10/1/2][S]

MITCHELL, BERNARD, born 1 Sept., bapt. 16 Nov. 1823, 4th son of David Mitchell, a labourer, born in Laurencekirk, Kincardineshire, and his wife Mary, dau. of Peter Matthews, a Customs officer in Penzance, Cornwall, England. [E]

MITCHELL, DAVID, a bachelor in Dundee, and Isabel Gray or Scott, a widow in Dundee, were married in her house in Perth Road, Dundee, 4 Mar. 1828. [S]

MITCHELL, DAVID, a bachelor in Dundee, and Elizabeth Miller, a spinster in Dundee, were married in her father's house in High Street, Dundee on 14 Sep. 1828. [S]

MITCHELL, DAVID, a vestryman, St Paul's, Dundee, 1833.
[DCA.GD.EC.D10.1-3]

MITCHELL, ELIZABETH, a spinster in Barony parish, Glasgow, and Henry Jacques, a bachelor in Barony parish, Glasgow, were married in Dundee, 1 Dec. 1827. [S]

MITCHELL, EUPHEMIA, dau. of Sylvester Mitchell and Marianna his wife born 3 July, bapt. 9 July 1815. [S]

MITCHELL, HELEN, dau. of Peter Mitchell and Clementina Vaiche, born 4 Feb., bapt. 9 Feb. 1817. [S]

MITCHELL, HELEN, a widow in Dundee, and James Gourlay, a bachelor in Dundee, were married in the house of Miss Greig, Forebank, Dundee, 14 Dec. 1828. [S]

MITCHEL, JAMES, son of Samuel Mitchel and Janet Lumsdale, born 24 Nov. 1816, bap. 2 Feb. 1817. [S]

MITCHELL, JAMES, a member of the Scots Episcopalian Church, Castle Street, Dundee, 1824. [DCA.GD.EC.D10.1/3]

MITCHELL, JANE, born 13 June, bapt. 22 July 1822, dau. of Helen Mitchell dau. of William Mitchell, a tailor in Dundee. [E]

MITCHELL, JANET, relict of Thomas Mitchell merchant, residing in High Street, Dundee, born 1737, died 21 Nov. 1808. [E]

MITCHELL, JANET, dau. of Sylvester Mitchell and Maia, his wife, born 4 July, bapt. 22 July 1813. [S]

MITCHELL, MARGARET, a spinster in Dundee, and James McNabb, a bachelor in Dundee, were married in the vestry of St Paul's, Castle Street, Dundee, 27 May 1828. [S]

MITCHELL, MARY, wife of George Fullarton, church member, 1764. [DCA.GD/EC/DIO/2/1]

MITCHELL, NELLY, dau. of John Mitchell and Nelly his wife, born 12 June, bapt. 13 Aug. 1815. [S]

MITCHELL, PETER, son of Peter Mitchell and Clementina Nairn, born 17 Sept, bapt. 24 Sept. 1815. [S]

MITCHELL, ROSE, dau. of Sylvester Mitchell and Marianna his wife, born 3 July, bapt. 9 July 1815. [S]

MITCHELL, S., and his wife, members of the Scots Episcopal Chapel, Castle Street, Dundee, 1824. [DCA.GD.EC.D10.1/3]

MITCHELL, THOMAS, 1743, a merchant, vestryman of the QEC, 1769; 1776. [DCA:GD/EC/D10] [DCA.GD/EC/DIO/2/1; 2/3]

MITCHELL, THOMAS, a bachelor in Dundee, and Graham [sic] Birnie, a spinster in Dundee, were married in the vestry of St Paul's, Castle Street, Dundee, 17 June 1831. [S]

MITCHELL, WILLIAM, a merchant, church member, 1777. [DCA:GD/EC/D10/1/2][S]

MITCHELL, WILLIAM, among the 'poor of Mr Hetherton's congregation, Dundee, 1830. [DCA.GD.EC.D10.1-3]

MITCHELL, Mrs, member of the QEC, 1776. [DCA:GD/EC/D10/1/1]

MITCHELL, Miss, a member of the Scots Episcopal Chapel, Castle Street, Dundee, 1824. [DCA.GD.EC.D10.1/3]

MOFFAT, ISOBEL, dau. of William Moffat in the Grounds of Balgay, Dundee, was bapt. 21 Jan. 1726. [BN]

MOFFAT, WILLIAM, son of William Moffat in the Grounds of Balgay, Dundee, was bapt. 10 Mar. 1724. [BN]

MOIR, AGNES, dau. of Charles Moir and Jane Robinson, born 6 Aug, bapt. 21 Aug 1814. [S]

MOIR, GRACE, born 22 Oct., bapt. 1 Nov. 1817, fifth dau. of James Moir, a shoemaker, born in Aberdeen, and his wife Euphemia, dau. of David Walker, a merchant in Montrose, Angus. [E]

MOLT, WILLIAM, a soldier of the 4th Royal Veteran Battalion, and Mary Head, were married 21 Feb.1820. [E]

MONCUR, ANDREW, pensioner, 1739. [DCA.GD/EC/DIO/2/1]

MONRO, ALEXANDER, son of Finlay Monro and Christian his wife, born 3 Nov, bapt. 12 Nov. 1815.[S]

MONRO, JOHN, son of Finlay Monro and Christian his wife, born 20 Jan, bapt. 31 Jan. 1813. [S]

MONRO, JOHN, a widower in Dundee, and Margaret Gordon, a spinster in Dundee, married in the house of James Robb, Castle Street Dundee, 4 July 1831. [S]

MONRO, MARGARET, 1st dau of Alexander Monro, the toll-keeper at Rathillet, Fife, born in Istradoun, Banffshire, and his wife Elizabeth, dau. of John Keith, a shepherd, born in Forgan, Fife born 9 Mar, bapt. 13 Apr. 1809. [E]

MONRO, MARGARET, born 19 Apr., bapt. 27 Apr.1823, 4th dau. of Peter Munro, a labourer, born in Inverness, and his wife Janet, dau. of Donald Macintosh in Inverness. [E]

MONTGOMERY, JAMES, member of the QEC, 1811. [DCA:GD/EC/D10/1/1]

MONTGOMERY, MARGARET HILL, 1st dau. of James Montgomery, a brewer at Pleasance, Dundee, born in Glasgow, and his wife Elizabeth, dau. of William Hackney, a merchant in Dundee, born 25 Dec. 1809, bapt. 12 Jan 1810. [E]

MONTGOMERY, ..., a vestryman, 1828/1835. [E] [DCA.GD.EC.D10.1-3]

MOODIE, ALEXANDER WEBSTER, son of John Moodie and Euphemia Meldrum, born 26 Dec. 1814, bapt. 28 May 1815. [S]

MOODIE, or MUDIE, ISOBELL, pensioner, 1739, 1742. [DCA.GD/EC/DIO/2/1]

MOORE, EUPHAM, pensioner, 1740. [DCA.GD/EC/DIO/2/1]

MOORE, ISABELLA, dau. of Robert Moore and his wife Isabel, born 22 Dec. 1816. [S]

MOORE, JANET BRUCE, 3rd dau of William Moore, a weaver, born in Glamis, Angus, and his wife Sarah, dau. of Henry Shanks, a labourer in Dundee, born 15 Oct, bapt. 29 Oct 1815. [E]

MOORE, MARGARET, 3rd dau. of George Moore, a Private of the 79th Regiment of Foot, born in Haddington, East Lothian, and his wife Dorothy, dau. of William Bennet, a shoemaker in Munster Haven, Ireland, born 18 July, bapt. 4 Aug. 1811. [E]

MOORE, PETER, 1st son of Peter Moore, a Sergeant of the 79th Regiment of Foot, born in Ayr, Ayrshire, and his wife Margaret Holmshaw, an innkeeper in Sheffield, Yorkshire, England, born 19 Oct, bapt. 21 Oct. 1810. [E]

MOORE, WILLIAM, son of Robert Moore and Isabel his wife, born 30 Jan, bapt. 25 Feb. 1815. [S]

MORE, ANDREW, member of the QEC, 1776. [DCA:GD/EC/D10/1/1]

MORE, or MOIR, JAMES, a bookseller and stationer, treasurer and vestryman of the QEC, 1757, 1764, 1768; 1776. [DCA:GD/EC/D10/1/1] [DCA.GD/EC/D10/2/2][E]

MOREHAM, ANNE, dau. of George Moreham and Anna Eason, born 5 Nov, bapt. 19 Nov. 1815. [S]

MORRICE, ANDREW, and his wife, members of the Scots Episcopal Chapel, Castle Street, Dundee, 1824. [DCA.GD.EC.D10.1/3]

MORRICE, JOHN, church member, 1781. [DCA.GD/EC/D10/1/2][S]

MORICE, WILLIAM, in Dundee, 1727. [ECD]; church member, 1743. [DCA.GD/EC/DIO/2/1; 2/3]

MORRISON, Captain ANDREW, a merchant in Dundee, 1727. [ECD]

MORRISON, JOHN NORMAN, son of John Whiteford Morrison, a Captain of the 1st Battalion of the 79th Regiment, and Sarah, his wife was born 21 Sept. bapt. 29 Oct. 1815. [S]

MORRISON, WILLIAM, member of the QEC, 1776. [DCA:GD/EC/D10/1/1]

MUAT, JOHN, a confectioner, and Margaret Peckman, both in Dundee, were married 29 Mar.1822.

MUDIE, JAMES, a weaver, church member, 1777. [DCA:GD/EC/D10/1/2][S]

MUDIE, MARY, in Dundee, and William Rymer in Dundee, were married in the house of Rev. John Hetherton, Paton's Lane, Dundee, 28 Nov. 1831. [S]

MUIR, ROBERT, son of Robert Muir and Elizabeth Ramsay, born 21 Aug. bapt. 12 Sept. 1813. [S]

MUNRO, JOHN, 1st son of William Munro, a drummer of the 79th Regiment of Foot, born in Golspie, Sutherland, and his wife Mary, dau. of John Andrew, a mariner in Falkirk, Stirlingshire, born 11 Nov, bapt. 19 Nov. 1815. [E]

MURPHY, JANE, dau. of Daniel Murphy and Margaret Geary, born 4 May, bapt. 14 Aug. 1814. [S]

MURPHY, SAMUEL, born 23 June, bapt. 21 Oct. 1829, 2nd son of James Murphy, a weaver, born in Bohoevie, County Londonderry, Ireland, and his wife Martha, dau. of Francis Shearer, a weaver in Connor, Ireland. [E]

MURRAY, BARBARA, dau of James Murray and Anne Blair, born 4 June, bapt. 13 Aug. 1815. [S]

MURRAY, DAVID, church member, 1743. [DCA.GD/EC/DIO/2/1; 2/3]

MURRAY, Dr GEORGE, of Invergowrie, Perthshire, vestryman, QEC, 1757; 1768; 1776. [DCA:GD/EC/D10/1/1] [DCA.GD/EC/D10/2/2][E]

MURRAY, JOHN, son of Henry Murray in Dundee, was bapt. 8 May 1723, godfathers were Westhall and Andrew Ogilvy of Templehall, with lady Westhall as godmother. [BN]

MURRAY, WILLIAM, a tailor in Dundee, 1727. [ECD]; church member, 1743. [DCA.GD/EC/DIO/2/1; 2/3]

MYLES, DAVID, church member, 1784. [DCA.GD/EC/D10/2/2][E]

MYLNE, AGNES, a spinster in Monifieth, Angus, residing in St George's parish, Edinburgh, and Charles Kinloch, of the parish of Gourdie, Perthshire, residing in St Andrew's parish, Edinburgh, were married at the house of Mrs Mackay, North Castle Street, Edinburgh, 25 July 1822. [S]

MYLNE, JOHN, son of John Mylne and May Donaldson, born 19 Oct, bapt. 31 Oct. 1813. [S]

MYLNE, MARGARET, dau. of Saunders Mylne and Elizabeth his wife born 5 Apr, bapt. 9 Apr 1815. [S]

MYLNE, JEAN, a spinster in Dundee, and William Duncanson, a bachelor in Alloa, Clackmannanshire, were married in the house of Rev. H. Horsley Magdalene Yard, Perth Road, Dundee, 1 Dec. 1835. [S]

NAIRN, CATHERINE, dau. of Alexander Nairn and Janet Chisholm, born 14 Apl., bapt. 12 May 1816. [S]

NAIRN, DAVID, of Drumkilbo, QEC committee, 1757. [DCA:GD/EC/D10/1/1] [DCA.GD/EC/D10/2/2][E]

NAIRN, JAMES, son of John Nairn and Helen Lawson, born 26 Mar, bapt. 16 May 1813. [S]

NAIRNE, Sir WILLIAM, church member,1743. [DCA.GD/EC/DIO/2/1]

NAIRN, WILLIAM, of Dunsinnan, Perthshire, church member, 1784. [DCA.GD/EC/D10/2/2][E]

NAIRN,......., of Baldovan, Dundee, 1727. [ECD]

NAPIER, MARY JANE, dau. of Alexander Napier and Mary Ann his wife born 25 Jan. 1816, bapt. 7 Feb. 1817. [S]

NASH, JAMES, Captain of the 6th Regiment of Foot, a widower, and Janet Ritchie, both in Dundee, were married 12 Dec. 1813. [S]

NAVAY, in 1743. [DCA.GD/EC/DIO/2/1]

NAWDON, THOMAS, organist of the QEC, pre1784. [DCA:GD/EC/D10/1/1]

NEAVE, ISOBEL, pensioner, 1740. [DCA.GD/EC/DIO/2/1]

NEILL, MARIA FOX, born 1 Apr., bapt. 22 Apr.1827, 2nd dau. of Thomas Neill, Chief Officer of the Coast Guard at Broughty Ferry, Angus, born in Ratho, Midlothian, and his wife Margaret, dau. of William Napier Customs Controller at Prestonpans, East Lothian. [E]

NEILSON, SAMUEL, and Mary Carrie, both in Dundee, were married in the house of Rev. John Hetherton, Paton's Lane, Dundee, 11 Nov. 1834. [S]

NEILSON, Mrs, member of the QEC, 1776. [DCA:GD/EC/D10/1/1]

NEISH, ALEXANDER, in Dundee, 1727. [ECD]

NEVIN, MARGARET, dau. of Daniel Nevin and Agnes his wife, born 5 Apl., bapt. 28 Apl. 1816. [S]

NICHOLSON, THOMAS, manager of the Railway Company, and Margaret Hill Kerr, were married at the house of Mrs Kerr, Tay Street, Dundee, 20 Oct. 1834. [S]; a vestryman, St Paul's, Dundee, 1835. [DCA.GD.EC.D10.1-3]

NICOLL, Mrs B., a member of the Scots Episcopal Chapel, Castle Street, Dundee, 1824. [DCA.GD.EC.D10.1/3]

NICOLL, DAVID, pensioner, 1739. [DCA.GD/EC/DIO/2/1]

NICOLL, DAVID, and Isabella Key, both of Dundee, were married in the vestry of St Paul's, Dundee, 20 Dec. 1833. [S]

NICOLL, GEORGE, session clerk, 1814, 1815. [E]

NICOLL, GILBERT, a pensioner aged 74 in 1818. [S] [DCA.GD.EC.D10.1/2]

NICOLL, JAMES, a bachelor in Dundee, and Margaret Watt, a spinster in Dundee, were married in the house of Rev. H. Horsley, Magdalene Road, Dundee, 11 Mar. 1836. [S]

NICOLL, JAMES, a bachelor in Dundee, and Margaret Watt, a spinster in Dundee, were married in the house of Rev. H. Horsley, Magdalene Road, Dundee, 11 Mar. 1836. [S]

NICOLL, THOMAS, and his wife, members of the Scots Episcopal Chapel, Castle Street, Dundee, 1824; a vestryman, 1825/1828/1830. [DCA.GD.EC.D10.1/3]

NICOLL, WILLIAM, son of William Nicoll and Margaret Fea, born 21 July, bapt. 7 Aug. 1814. [S]

NIMMO, ALEXANDER DUNCAN, 2nd son of Patrick Nimmo a surgeon, born in Dundee, and his wife Margaret Johnston Duncan, dau. of Alexander Duncan DD, vicar of Bolam, Northumberland, England, born 6 Nov., bapt. 4 Dec. 1814. [E]

NIMMO, GEORGINA, born 6 May, bapt. 1 June 1827, 4th dau. of Patrick Nimmo, a surgeon, born in Dundee, and his wife Margaret Johnston, dau. of the late Rev. Alexander Duncan, Rector of Whalton, Northumberland, England. [E]

NIMMO, HELEN MACLEAN, dau. of Patrick Nimmo, a surgeon, born in Dundee, and his wife Margaret Johnston Duncan, dau. of Alexander Duncan, vicar of Bolam, Northumberland, England, born 20 June, bapt. 4 July 1813. [E]

NIMMO, JAMES JOHNSTON DUNCAN, born 26 Dec. 1819, bapt. 30 Jan. 1820, 4th son of Patrick Nimmo a surgeon, born in Dundee, and his wife Margaret Johnston, dau. of Rev. Alexander Duncan DD, Vicar of Bolam, Rector of Whalton, Northumberland, England. [E]

NIMMO, JOHN MACDONALD, born 29 Nov., bapt. 26 Dec. 1824, 5th son of Patrick Nimmo, MD a surgeon, born in Dundee, and his wife Margaret Johnston, dau. of Rev. Alexander Duncan DD, Vicar of Bolam, Rector of Whalton, Northumberland, England. [E]

NIMMO, JOHNSTON PILLAN, born 28 Oct. 1821, bapt. 24 Nov. 1821, 5th son of Patrick Nimmo, MD a surgeon, born in Dundee, and his wife Margaret Johnston, dau. of Rev. Alexander Duncan DD, Vicar of Bolam, Rector of Whalton, Northumberland, England. [E]

NIMMO, MARGARET JOHNSTON, 1st dau of Patrick Nimmo, a surgeon, born in Dundee, and his wife Margaret Johnston Duncan, dau. of Alexander Duncan, vicar of Bolam, Northumberland, England, born 19 Nov., bapt. 8 Dec. 1811. [E]

NIMMO, MARIA, born 29 Jan., bapt. 22 Feb. 1818, dau. of Patrick Nimmo, a surgeon, born in Dundee, and his wife Margaret Johnston, dau. of the late Rev. Alexander Duncan, Rector of Whalton, Northumberland, England. [E]

NIMMO, PATRICK, 1st son of Patrick Nimmo, a surgeon, born in Dundee, and his wife Margaret Johnston Duncan, dau. of Alexander Duncan, vicar of Bolam, Northumberland, England, born 4 Aug, bapt. 12 Aug. 1810. [E]

NIMMO, THOMAS MILLER, born 12 May, bapt. 8 June 1823, 6th son of Patrick Nimmo a surgeon, born in Dundee, and his wife Margaret Johnston, dau. of Rev. Alexander Duncan DD, Vicar of Bolam, Rector of Whalton, Northumberland, England. [E]

NIMMO, PATRICK, 1st son of Patrick Nimmo, a surgeon, born in Dundee, and his wife Margaret Johnston Duncan, dau of Alexander Duncan, vicar of Bolam, Northumberland, England, born 4 Aug., bapt. 12 Aug. 1810. [E]

NISBET, Mrs, pensioner, 1739. [DCA.GD/EC/DIO/2/1]

NOBLE, GEORGE, born 25 May, bapt. 5 June 1825, 1st son of John Noble, a weaver, born in Dungorton, County Tyrone, Ireland, and his wife Margaret, dau. of George Anderson a brewer in Dundee. [E]

NOBLE, JAMES, born 11 Mar., bapt. 25 Mar. 1827, 2nd son of John Noble, a weaver, born in Dungorton, County Tyrone, Ireland, and his wife Margaret, dau. of George Anderson a brewer in Dundee. [E]

NOBLE, SARAH, born 9 Feb., bap. 22 Feb. 1829, 1st dau. of John Noble a weaver, born in Dungorton, County Tyrone, Ireland, and his wife Margaret, dau. of George Anderson a brewer in Dundee. [E]

NORRIE, ROBERT, minister of St Paul's, Dundee, from 1689 to 1727, graduated MA from St Andrews, University, in 1667, Minister of Dunfermline, Fife, from 1686 until deprived by the Privy Council in 1689 as a Jacobite, he was consecrated a Bishop of the Nonjurant Church at Edinburgh in 1724. Bishop of Brechin. He died in 1727 aged about 80. He married Isabel, eldest dau. of John Guthrie of Westhall, Angus. [F.5.320][S]

NORRIS, MARY, born 11 Sep. bapt. 12 Nov. 1820, 2nd dau. of Samuel Norris, a travelling chapman born in Glasgow, and his wife Ann, dau. of Henry Gibson a horn-spoon maker in Edinburgh. [E]

NOTT, MARY, dau. of Thomas Nott and Magdalen Hutchinson, born 10 May, bapt. 8 Aug. 1813. [S]

NOWLES, ISABELLA ESTHER, 3rd dau of Lieutenant Abraham Nowles of the 25th Regiment of Foot, born in Berwick-on-Tweed, Northumberland, England, and his wife Ann, dau. of Charles Allison in Berwick –on-Tweed, born 16 Dec. 1809, bapt. 17 Jan. 1810. [E]

NUCATOR, ALEXANDER, 1st son of Andrew Nucator, gardener of Chapelshade, Dundee, born in Dundee, and his wife Margaret, dau. of Patrick Murray, a farmer in Foulis, Angus, born 5 Mar., bapt 10 Mar. 1811. [E]

NUCATOR, ANDREW, born 14 Jan., bap. 20 Feb. 1825, 3rd son of John Nucator, a gardener born in Dundee, and his wife Mary, dau. of Samuel Bromley, a labourer in Dundee. [E]

NUCATOR, DAVID BLAIR, born 23 Sept., bap. 3 Oct. 1819, first son of John Nucator, a gardener born in Dundee, and his wife Mary, dau. of Samuel Bromley, a labourer in Dundee. [E]

NUCATOR, ELIZABETH, dau. of Andrew Nucator, gardener of Chapelshade, Dundee, born in Dundee, and his wife Margaret, dau. of Patrick Murray, a farmer, born in Foulis, Angus, born 4 June, bapt. 11 June 1809. [E]

NUCATOR, JOHN THOMSON, born 18 Feb. bapt. 2 Mar. 1823, 2nd son of Andrew Nucator, gardener of Chapelshade, Dundee, born in Dundee, and his wife Margaret, dau. of Patrick Murray, a farmer, born in Foulis, Angus, born 4 June, bapt. 11 June 1809. [E]

O'BRIAN, JOHN, born 21 June, bapt. 27 July 1828, 6th son of Joseph O'Brian, a flax-dresser, born in Sandfield, County Down, Ireland, and his wife Elizabeth, dau. of ... Hamilton a labourer in Templepatrick, County Antrim, Ireland. [E]

OGILVIE, AGNES, born 31 May, bapt. 7 June 1817, 2nd dau. of David Ogilvie, a ships carpenter, born in Dundee, and his wife Margaret, dau. of Thomas Chalmers in Dundee. [E]

OGILVIE, ALEXANDER, a surgeon, vestryman and treasurer of the QEC, 1778, 1810. [DCA:GD/EC/D10/1/1]

OGILVIE, ANN, a member of the Scots Episcopal Chapel, Castle Street, Dundee, 1824. [DCA.GD.EC.D10.1/3]

OGILVY, CLEMENTINA, a spinster in Dundee, and John Baillie, a bachelor in Dundee, were married in the vestry of St Paul's, Castle Street, Dundee, on 13 Nov. 1828. [S]

OGILVIE, DAVID, 1st son of David Ogilvie, a ships carpenter, born in Dundee, and his wife Margaret, dau of Thomas Chalmers, born in Dundee, born 7 Oct, bapt. 13 Oct. 1811. [E]

OGILVIE, GEORGE, of Baikie, Angus, a vestryman of the QEC, 1780, 1784. [DCA:GD/EC/D10/1/1][DCA.GD/EC/D10/2/2][E]

OGILVIE, GUSTAVUS, church member, 1764. [DCA.GD/EC/DIO/2/1]

OGILVIE, HENRY, church member, 1758. [DCA.GD/EC/D10/2/2][E] [a Jacobite in 1745]

OGILVIE, JAMES, of Ruthven, Angus, vestryman of the QEC, 1781, 1784. [DCA:GD/EC/D10/1/1] [DCA.GD/EC/D10/2/2][E]

OGILVIE, JANE, 1st dau. of David Ogilvie, a ships carpenter, born in Dundee, and his wife Margaret, dau. of Thomas Chalmers, born in Dundee, born 17 Jan. bapt. 27 Jan. 1809. [E]

OGILVY, JANET, pensioner, 1739. [DCA.GD/EC/DIO/2/1]

OGILVY, Sir JOHN, of Inverarity, Angus, QEC committee, 1757; vestryman 1764; 1776. [DCA:GD/EC/D10/1/1] [DCA.GD/EC/D10/2/2][E]

OGILVIE, JOHN, 2nd son of David Ogilvie, a ships carpenter, born in Dundee, and his wife Margaret, dau. of Thomas Chalmers, born in Dundee, born 26 Nov. bapt. 5 Dec 1813. [E]

OGILVY, MARGARET, dau of .... Ogilvy of Westhall, was bapt. 9 Apr. 1724, the godfather was the laird of Monorgan, Perthshire, while godmothers were the wife of Thomas Crichton, a surgeon apothecary in Dundee and Mrs James Pilmor, dau. of the Lady Dowager of Monorgan. [BN]

OGILVY, MARGARET, dau. of Henry Ogilvy of Templehall, Angus, a merchant in Dundee, was bapt. 25 June 1726. [BN]

OGILVIE, Miss MARY, a member of the Scots Episcopal Chapel, Castle Street, Dundee, 1824. [DCA.GD.EC.D10.1/3]

OGILVIE, Miss M., a member of the Scots Episcopal Chapel, Castle Street, Dundee, 1824. [DCA.GD.EC.D10.1/3]

OGILVY, THOMAS, son of Henry Ogilvy of Templehall, Angus, was bapt. in his house in the Murraygait, Dundee, on 2 June 1724. [BN]

OGILVY, THOMAS FOTHERINGHAM, of Powrie, Angus, QEC committee, 1757. [DCA:GD/EC/D10/1/1]

OGILVIE, Dr, member QEC, 1776. [DCA:GD/EC/D10/1/1]

OGILVIE, Dr, vestryman, 1807. [DCA.GD/EC/D10/1/2][S]

OGILVIE, Miss, (1), member of the QEC, 1776. [DCA:GD/EC/D10/1/1]

OGILVIE, Miss, (2), member of the QEC, 1776. [DCA:GD/EC/D10/1/1]

OGILVY, Mrs, pensioner, 1739. [DCA.GD/EC/DIO/2/1]

OGILVIE,......, of Ruthven, Angus, member of the QEC, 1776, 1779. [DCA:GD/EC/D10/1/1]

OLIPHANT, Mrs, member of the QEC, 1776. [DCA:GD/EC/D10/1/1]

OREM, ALEXANDER, son of Alexander Orem and Elizabeth Angus, born 4 Feb., bapt. 14 July 1816. [S]

ORAM, ROSANNA, 2nd dau. of James Oram, a labourer, born in Forgan, Fife, and his wife Catharine, dau. of George Miller, a shoemaker in Forgan, Fife, born 5 May, bapt. 15 May 1815. [E]

ORCHART, WILLIAM, a ropemaker, church member, 1764, 1777, 1781. [DCA:GD/EC/D10/1/2][S]

OUCHTERLONY, ANDREW, church member, 1743. [DCA.GD/EC/DIO/2/1; 2/3]

OUCHTERLONY, DAVID, a merchant, church member, 1777, treasurer 1781; 1810. [DCA:GD/EC/D10/1/2][S]

OUCHTERLONY, DAVID, a vestryman, 1817/1818/1819/1820/1825. [S][DCA.GD.EC.D10.1/2/3]

OCHTERLONY, JOHN, at St Paul's, Dundee, from 1726 to 1727; at the Seagait Chapel, Dundee, from 1727 until 1742. [possibly son of John Ochterlony, minister of Balmerino, Fife, from 1682 until 1690, born 1707]

OVENSTONE, ISABEL, pensioner, 1740. [DCA.GD/EC/DIO/2/1]

PARKER, ELIZABETH, dau. of William Parker and Janet Gilchrist, born 4 Jan., bapt. 26 May 1816. [S]

PARKINS, WILLIAM, son of William Parkins and Janet Gilchrist, born 6 Oct. 1813, bapt. 8 Apr. 1814. [S]

PATERSON, CATHERINE, dau. of Charles Paterson and Catherine his wife, born 21 June, bapt. 4 Oct. 1812. [S]

PATERSON, GEORGE, of Castle Huntly, vestryman of the QEC, 1781, 1784. [DCA:GD/EC/D10/1/1] [DCA.GD/EC/D10/2/2][E]

PATERSON, Dr JAMES, QEC vestryman, 1768. [DCA:GD/EC/D10/1/1]

PATTERSON, JANET, dau. of Archibald Patterson and Sally his wife born 28 Aug, bapt. 17 Sept 1815. [S]

PATTERSON, JOHN, 3rd son of John Patterson, a weaver, born in Forgan, Fife, and his wife Catherine, dau. of John Eaton, a mason in Brechin, Angus, born 11 Nov. bapt. 19 Nov. 1809. [E]

PATERSON, MARGARET, pensioner, 1745. [DCA.GD/EC/D10/2/1]

PATERSON, Lady CRAIGIE, (sic), church member, 1746, 1750. [DCA.GD/EC/D10/2/1]

PATTERSON, SUSAN, dau. of John Patterson and Anne Rattray, born 24 May, bapt 11 June 1815. [S]

PATERSON, Mrs THOMAS, church member, 1746. [DCA.GD/EC/D10/2/1]

PAUL, ANNE, dau. of William Paul and Anne Morison, born 10 Aug, bapt. 2 Oct. 1814. [S]

PAUL, HUGH CAMPBELL, a merchant in Glasgow, and Isabella Livingston in Dundee, were married 23 Apr. 1823. [E]

PEARSON, ALEXANDER, church member, 1764. [DCA.GD/EC/DIO/2/1]

PEARSON, DAVID, in Dundee, and Mary Wishart in Arbroath, Angus, were married, 13 Jan. 1818. [E]

PEAT, WILLIAM, son of John Peat and Janet Porter, born 26 Jan., bapt. 27 Mar. 1816. [S]

PEEBLES, BETSEY, dau. of James Peebles and Ellen his wife, born 31 May, bapt. 4 June 1814. [S]

PEEBLES, JANET, dau. of James Peebles and Ellen his wife, born 6 Nov, bap. 1 Dec. 1816. [S]

PETER, HELEN, born 24 May, bapt. 11 June 1826, 2nd dau of David Peter, born in Dundee, a Private of the 91st Regiment of Foot, and his wife Jane, daughter of James Galloway, a slater in Dundee. [E]

PETERKIN, DAVID, son of Isaac Peterkin and Charlotte his wife, bapt June 1815. [S]

PETRIE, GEORGINA JUSTICE, born 1 Mar., bapt. 21 Mar. 1828, 1st dau. of James Petrie, inn-keeper, born in Monikie, Angus, and his wife Ann, dau. of Philip Rich, a wheeler and carpenter in Marylebone, London. [E]

PETRIE, JOHN, a clergyman, pensioner, 1740. [DCA.GD/EC/DIO/2/1]

PETTY, SUSANNA, dau. of John Petty and Susan Campbell, born 1 Aug., bapt. 11 Aug. 1816. [S]

PHILIPS, JOHN, son of John Philips, a Private of the 91st Regiment and Janet Bodie, born 17 Nov. 1811, bapt. 24 Jan. 1812. [S]

PHILLIPS, Dr, member of the QEC, 1776. [DCA:GD/EC/D10/1/1]

PHILLIPS, Major, member of the QEC, 1811. [DCA:GD/EC/D10/1/1]

PHIN, LILIAS, a spinster in Dundee, married John Kennedy, a bachelor in Dundee, in her father's house in the Overgait, Dundee, 16 July 1827. [S]

PHINN, ..., a pensioner, 1739. [DCA.GD/EC/DIO/2/1]

PIERSON, WILLIAM MACKAY, born 24 Apr. 1804, bapt. 17 Aug. 1823, son of Euphemia Pierson, a single-woman, daughter of ..... Pierson in Salton, Lothian. [E]

PINCHBACK, ELIZABETH, wife of John Jolly a druggist in Dundee, born 1761, died 21 Aug. 1809. [E]

PIRRIE, MARGARET, member of the QEC, 1776. [DCA:GD/EC/D10/1/1]

PIRRIE, Mrs, pensioner, 1739. [DCA.GD/EC/DIO/2/1]

PITCAIRN, Dr, a member of the Scots Episcopal Chapel, Castle Street, Dundee, 1824. [DCA.GD.EC.D10.1/3]

PITKEATHLY, ANNA, born 15 Dec. 1821, bapt. 13 Jan. 1822, 1st dau. of Robert Pitkeathly, a mariner, born in Newburgh, Fife, and his wife Janet, dau. of John Wishart, a mariner in Dundee. [E]

POPE, DAVID, organist, 1817/1818. [S][DCA.GD.EC.D10.1/2]

PORTER, AILES GRIFFITHS, dau. of John Porter and Ellen his wife, born 2 June, bapt. 9 July 1815. [S]

PORTER, JAMES, son of Peter Porter and Jane Dixon, born 28 Jan., bapt. 18 Feb. 1816. [S]

PRICE, JOHN, born 6 June, bapt. 25 June 1820, first son of Edward Price, born in Clennis, County Fermanagh, Ireland, a Private of the 8th Veteran Battalion, and his wife Ann, dau. of John Gutheridge, a farmer in Rossory, County Fermanagh, Ireland. [E]

PRINGLE, JAMES, son of James Pringle and his wife Anne, born 16 June, bapt. 30 June 1811. [S]

PUSSEY, ELIZABETH ANN, 1st dau of James Pussey, a steward on the Dundee & London smack <u>Defiance</u>, born in Edinburgh, and his wife Ann, dau. of John Andrew a farmer in Clapham, Surrey, born 4 Oct, bapt. 20 Dec. 1815. [E]

PYET, JAMES, member of the QEC, 1776. [DCA:GD/EC/D10/1/1]

RAIT, ASHLEY, son of James Rait and Jane Low his wife, born 6 June, bapt. 6 Sept. 1812. [S]

RAIT, BARBARA, pensioner, 1739. [DCA.GD/EC/DIO/2/1]

RAITT, Captain CHARLES, and his wife, members of the Scots Episcopal Chapel, Castle Street, Dundee, 1824/1828; a vestryman, 1825/1830/1835. [DCA.GD.EC.D10.1/3]

RAIT, DAVID, son of David Rait in Wallace of Craigie, was bapt. 16 Oct. 1726. [BN]

RAITT, DAVID, 1739. [DCA.GD/EC/DIO/2/1]

RAITT, GEORGE, a merchant, church member, 1777. [DCA:GD/EC/D10/1/2][S]

RAIT, JAMES, minister, 1727-1777. [ECD][DCA:GD/EC/D10/1/2][S]

RAIT, JOHN, son of David Rait in Wallace of Craigie, Angus, was bapt. 3 Jan. 1725. [BN]

RAITT, JOHN, of Anniston, Angus, vestryman of the QEC, 1781, 1784. [DCA:GD/EC/D10/1/1] [DCA.GD/EC/D10/2/2][E]

RAIT, ROBERT, possibly born in Brechin, Angus, about 1651, son of Reverend William Rait, graduated MA from St Andrews 1672, minister of St Paul's from 1682 until deprived by the Privy Council 1689, he died in 1704. He married Elizabeth, dau. of Alexander Wedderburn of Kingennie, Angus, and Easter Powrie, Angus, in 1684, parents of Alexander. He died in 1704. [F.5.331][S]

RAIT, Dr, 1743, [DCA.GD/EC/DIO/2/1; 2/3]

RAITT, Bishop, and Mrs Rait, church members, 1764. [DCA.GD/EC/DIO/2/1]

RAMSAY, DAVID, a merchant, vestryman of the QEC, 1768 [DCA:GD/EC/D10/1/1]

RAMSAY, DAVID, a merchant, vestryman, 1802; 1810.
[DCA.GD/EC/D10/1/2][S]

RAMSAY, GEORGE, church member, 1743. [DCA.GD/EC/DIO/2/1; 2/3]

RAMSAY, HELEN, pensioner, 1740. [DCA.GD/EC/DIO/2/1]

RAMSAY, Miss H., a member of the Scots Episcopal Chapel, Castle Street, Dundee, 1824. [DCA.GD.EC.D10.1/3]

RAMSAY, JAMES, church member, 1764. [DCA.GD/EC/DIO/2/1]

RAMSAY, JAMES WEDDERBURN, son of James Ramsay and Ellen Archer, born 18 June, bapt. 23 July 1815. [S]

RAMSAY, JOHN, of Kinaly, church member, 1777.
[DCA:GD/EC/D10/1/2][S]

RAMSAY, JOHN, a widower in Dundee, and Mary Ann Bell, a spinster in Dundee, were married in St Paul's Castle Street, Dundee, 4 July 1830.

RAMSAY, ROBERT, a brewer, church member, 1743, 1746, 1750, 1758. [DCA.GD/EC/DIO/2/1] [DCA.GD/EC/D10/2/2; 2/3][E]

RAMSAY, ..., with two Misses Ramsay, members of the QEC, 1776.
[DCA:GD/EC/D10/1/1]

RAMSAY, Mrs, member of the QEC, 1776. [DCA:GD/EC/D10/1/1]

RAMSAY, the Misses, church members, 1810.
[DCA.GD/EC/D10/1/2]

RAMSAY, Miss, a member of the Scots Episcopal Chapel, Castle Street, Dundee, 1824/1828. [DCA.GD.EC.D10.1/3]

RANKINE, DAVID ROBERT, son of James Rankin and Judith his wife, born 6 Nov. 1813, bapt. 3 Jan 1814. [S]

RANKINE, Miss F., a member of the Scots Episcopal Chapel, Castle Street, Dundee, 1824. [DCA.GD.EC.D10.1/3]

RANKINE, JOHN, church member, 1758. [DCA.GD/EC/D10/2/2][E]

RANKINE, Miss N.E., a member of the Scots Episcopal Chapel, Castle Street, Dundee, 1824. [DCA.GD.EC.D10.1/3]

RANKINE, the Misses, of Dudhope, Dundee, church members, 1810.
[DCA.GD/EC/D10/1/2][S]

RANKINE, Miss, a member of the Scots Episcopal Chapel, Castle Street, Dundee, 1824. [DCA.GD.EC.D10.1/3]

RANSOM, FRANCIS, born 10 Aug., bapt. 3 Sept. 1820, second son of William Ransom, born in Dysartmartin, County Londonderry, Ireland, a Sergeant of the 8th Royal Veteran Battalion, and his wife Jane, dau. of Samuel Colwell, a surgeon in Dysartmartin, County Londonderry. [E]

RATTRAY, ALEXANDER, church member, 1781.
[DCA.GD/EC/D10/1/2][S]

RATTRAY, GEORGE, church member, 1764. [DCA.GD/EC/DIO/2/1]

RATTRAY, JAMES, a brewer, church member, 1743, 1746, 1750.
[DCA.GD/EC/DIO/2/1; 2/3]

RATTRAY, MARGARET, born 17 Feb., bapt. 13 Apr. 1828, 1st dau. of David Rattray, a seaman, born in Dundee, and his wife Elizabeth, dau. of David Grimmond, a porter in Dundee. [E]

RATTRAY, THOMAS, and his wife, members of the Scots Episcopal Chapel, Castle Street, Dundee, 1824. [DCA.GD.EC.D10.1/3]

RAYNE, ELSPIT, dau. of William Rayne and Elspit Melvill, born 19 Nov. bapt. 10 Dec. 1813. [S]

READ, Captain ALEXANDER, QEC committee, 1757; 1776.
[DCA:GD/EC/D10/1/1] [DCA.GD/EC/D10/2/2][E]

READ, ALEXANDER, of Logie, Dundee, vestryman of the QEC, 1781, 1784. [DCA:GD/EC/D10/1/1] [DCA.GD/EC/D10/2/2][E]

READ, ALEXANDER, born 17 Dec. bapt. 31 Dec. 1826, 2nd son of John Read, a coppersmith, born in Dundee, and his wife Margaret, dau. of William Mitchell, a tailor in Dundee. [E]

READ, Captain DAVID, member of the QEC, 1776.
[DCA:GD/EC/D10/1/1]

READ, DAVID, of Drumgeith, Angus, vestryman of the QEC, 1781, 1784. [DCA:GD/EC/D10/1/1] [DCA.GD/EC/D10/2/2][E]

READ, ELIZABETH, dau. of James Read and Jane his wife, born 18 Mar. bapt. 16 Apr. 1815. [S]

READ, Mrs FLETCHER, church member, 1810.
[DCA.GD/EC/D10/1/2][S]

READ, JAMES, pensioner, 1740. [DCA.GD/EC/DIO/2/1]

READ, JAMES, son of Alexander Read and Margaret his wife, born 20 Aug. bapt. 3 Sept 1815. [S]

READ, Captain JOHN, church member, 1758. [DCA.GD/EC/D10/2/2][E]

READ, THOMAS, church member, 1784. [DCA.GD/EC/D10/2/2]

READ, THOMAS ELLIS, born 23 May, bapt. 7 June 1824, 1st son of John Read, a coppersmith, born in Dundee, and his wife Margaret, dau. of William Mitchell, a tailor in Dundee. [E]

READ, WILLIAM, vestryman of the QEC, 1781, 1784. [DCA:GD/EC/D10/1/1] [DCA.GD/EC/D10/2/2][E]

READ, WILLIAM RATTRAY, son of John Read and his wife Anne, born 1 Aug., bapt. 18 Aug. 1816. [S]

READ, Miss, member of the QEC, 1776. [DCA:GD/EC/D10/1/1]

REAY, Mr, member of the QEC, 1776. [DCA:GD/EC/D10/1/1]

REID, ELIZABETH, dau. of Thomas Reid and Jessie Pennicuick, born 30 June, bapt. 28 July 1816. [S]

REID, JAMES, son of Andrew Reid and Anne his wife, born 3 Jan, bapt. 25 Jan. 1815. [S]

REID, JAMES, son of Daniel Reid and Anne his wife, born 26 Jan. bapt. 6 Feb. 1815. [S]

REID, JOHN, a coppersmith, and Margaret Mitchell, both in Dundee, were married 17 Nov. 1823. [E]

REID, MARGARET JANE, born 6 Mar., bapt. 10 Apr.1825, dau. of Euphemia Seaton, dau. of David Seaton, a butcher in Dundee. [E]

REID, MARIAN, dau. of John Reid and Bel Pitcairns, born 10 July, bapt. 24 July 1814. [S]

RENNIE, ..., a member of the Scots Episcopal Chapel, Castle Street, Dundee, 1824. [DCA.GD.EC.D10.1/3]

RICHIE, PETER, son of George Richie in Pitcarrow, Angus, bapt. 23 Mar. 1726. [BN]

RIGG, JOHN, church member, 1743. [DCA.GD/EC/DIO/2/1; 2/3]

RIND, GRISEL, dau. of David Rind in the Ground of Balgay, Dundee, bapt. 1 Feb. 1726. [BN]

RINGLAND, JAMES, 1st son of James Ringland, Sergeant of the 70th Regiment of Foot, born in Ochnacly, County Down, Ireland, and his wife Mary, dau. of Robert Harris labourer in Tarbolton, Ayrshire, born 26 May, bapt. 5 June 1814. [E]

RITCHIE, ALEXANDER, 6th son of John Ritchie, a shoemaker in Broughty Ferry, Angus, born in Panbride, Angus, and his wife Margaret, dau. of Andrew Bertram, a blacksmith, born in Dundee, born 26 Feb, bapt. 13 Apr. 1814. [E]

RITCHIE, ANDREW, born 6 May, bapt. 5 June 1816, son of John Ritchie, a shoemaker in Broughty Ferry, Angus, born in Panbride, Angus, and his wife Margaret Bertram, dau. of Andrew Bertram, a blacksmith in Dundee. [E]

RITCHIE, DAVID, 4th son of John Ritchie, a shoemaker in Broughty Ferry, Angus, born in Panbride, Angus, and his wife Margaret, dau. of Andrew Bertram, a blacksmith, born in Dundee, born 29 Jan. bapt. 19 Feb. 1809. [E]

RITCHIE, ISABELLA, 1st dau of David Ritchie, a Private of the 6th Battalion of the Artillery, born in Arbroath, Angus, and his wife Janet, dau. of Rowland Mitchell, a labourer in Dundee, born 29 Oct. bapt. 10 Nov. 1811. [E]

RITCHIE, JAMES, 5th son of John Ritchie, a shoemaker in Broughty Ferry, born in Panbride, Angus, and his wife Margaret, dau. of Andrew Bertram, born in Dundee, born 1 June, bapt. 18 June 1811. [E]

RITCHIE, JAMES, son of James Ritchie and Janet his wife, born 26 Nov. 1814, bapt. 6 Mar. 1815. [S]

RITCHIE, LIZZIE, church member, 1764. [DCA.GD/EC/DIO/2/1]

RITCHIE, PATRICK DALL, 1st son of Lieutenant William Ritchie of the Royal Navy, born in Panbride, Angus, and his wife Barbara, dau of George Dall, a farmer at Easthaven, Angus, born 2 Mar. bapt. 16 Mar. 1815. [E]

RITCHIE, PETER, born 31 Oct., bap. 5 Nov. 1818, son of John Ritchie, a shoemaker in Broughty Ferry, Angus, born in Panbride, Angus, and his wife Margaret Bertram, dau. of Andrew Bertram, a blacksmith in Dundee. [E]

RITCHIE, WILLIAM, born 4 Dec., bapt. 30 Dec. 1818, 2nd son of William Ritchie, a Lieutenant of the Royal Navy and master mariner of the merchant ship Amazon sailing from the port of London to Jamaica, born in Panbride, Angus, and his wife Barbara, dau. of the late George Dall, farmer in Easthaven, Angus. [E]

ROBB, ALLAN, son of David Robb and Margaret Gardiner, born 24 Apl., bapt. 5 May 1816. [S]

ROBB, CHARLES, born 8 Sep., bapt. 28 Oct.1827, 2nd son of Alexander Robb, a shoemaker, born in Forfar, Angus, and his wife Isabella, dau. of the late Robert Lowrie a tailor in Ratho, Midlothian. [E]

ROBB, Mrs, a widow, a pensioner aged 78 in 1818. [S][DCA.GD.EC.D10.1/2]

ROBERTS, AMELIA ELIZABETH, dau. of William Roberts and Margaret his wife, born 25 Apr, bapt. 29 May 1812. [S]

ROBERTS, ANNE, dau of William Roberts and Margaret his wife, born 15 Apr. bapt. 18 Dec. 1813. [S]

ROBERTS, CHARLES, minister of the Qualified Chapel in Dundee, from 1751 until 1768. [DCA:GD/EC/D10/1/1; 2/2[[E][DCA.RD29.866]

ROBERTS, ELEANOR, dau. of William Roberts and Margaret his wife, born 14 July, bapt. 10 Aug. 1816. [S]

ROBERTS, WILLIAM, a banker, church member, 1810. [DCA.GD/EC/D10/1/2][S]; a banker and vestryman, 1817/1818/1824. [S][DCA.GD.EC.D10.1/2/3]

ROBERTS, Mrs, member of the QEC, 1776. [DCA:GD/EC/D10/1/1]

ROBERTSON, AGNES ELLIS, dau. of David Robertson and Janet his wife, born 6 Feb, bapt. 6 Mar. 1813. [S]

ROBERTSON, ALEXANDER, 1743, merchant, vestryman QEC, 1764, 1768;1776; 1777. [DCA:GD/EC/D10/1/1][DCA.GD/EC/DIO/2/1; 2/3] [DCA.GD/EC/D10/2/2][E]

ROBERTSON, BETTY, dau. of Thomas Robertson and Betty his wife, born 10 Sept, bapt. 18 Sept. 1814. [S]

ROBERTSON, DUNCAN, merchant, church member, 1777. [DCA.GD/EC/D10/1/2][S]

ROBERTSON, ELIZABETH, in Dundee, and Andrew Small, in Dundee, were married in the house of John Robertson, Horsewater Wynd, Dundee, 5 Apl. 1832. [S]

ROBERTSON, HELEN, dau. of David Robertson and Elizabeth Peters, born 27 May, bapt. 30 June 1816. [S]

ROBERTSON, JAMES, a weaver, pensioner, 1739, 1742. [DCA.GD/EC/DIO/2/1]

ROBERTSON, JANE, born 22 July, bapt. 7 Oct. 1827, 2nd dau. of James Robertson, a weaver, born in Dowley, Perthshire, and his wife Elizabeth dau. of John Monaghan a labourer in Tullamore, King's County, Ireland. [E]

ROBERTSON, WILLIAM, of the Seagait Chapel in Dundee, from 1742 until 1743; at St Paul's, from 1743 until 1750.

ROBERTSON, Mrs, a member of the Scots Episcopal Chapel, Castle Street, Dundee, 1824. [DCA.GD.EC.D10.1/3]

ROBINSON, CHARLES, son of Alexander Robinson and Betsey Fraser, born 21 Mar. bapt. 25 Mar. 1815. [S]

ROBINSON, ELIZABETH, 2nd dau of William Robinson cast-iron founder, born in Tanfield, Durham, England, and his wife Jane, dau. of Andrew Whitlaw in Perth, born 21 Apr. bapt. 13 May 1810. [E]

ROBINSON, EUPHEMIA, dau. of Robert Robinson and Euphemia Keiller, born 1 Nov. bapt. 6 Dec. 1812. [S]

ROBINSON, GEORGE, born and bapt. 17 June 1823, 7th son of John Robinson, a weaver, born in Maghricross, County Fermanagh, Ireland, and his wife Mary, dau. of Francis Armstrong, a miller in Maghricross, County Fermanagh. [E]

ROBINSON, JAMES, born 7 Apl., bapt. 26 July 1818, 2nd son of William Robinson, a butcher born in Kilmany, Fife, and his wife Margaret, dau. of James Spink, a weaver in Dundee. [E]

ROBINSON, JOHN, son of Daniel Robertson and Lizzy Robinson, born 24 Oct. bapt. 13 Nov. 1814. [S]

ROBINSON, JOHN OGILVY, son of Alexander Robinson and Betsey Fraser, born 21 Mar. bapt. 25 Mar. 1815. [S]

ROBINSON, MARGARET, dau. of Alexander Robinson and his wife Rachelle, born 27 Dec. 1815, bapt. 7 Jan. 1816. [S]

ROBINSON, PETER, son of Peter Robinson and Grizel his wife, born 27 Sept. bapt. 22 Oct. 1815. [S]

ROBINSON, WILLIAM, born 29 June, bapt. 11 July 1828, 2nd son of Arthur Robinson, a weaver, born in Glasgow, and his wife Ann, dau. of the late Barnet Gillespie, a weaver in Glasgow. [E]

ROBINSON, Miss, member of the QEC, 1776. [DCA:GD/EC/D10/1/1]

ROBSON, THOMAS, vestryman of the QEC, 1778. [DCA:GD/EC/D10/1/1] [DCA.GD/EC/D10/2/2][E]

ROBSON, Captain, member of the QEC, 1776. [DCA:GD/EC/D10/1/1]

RODGER, CHARLES, son of Charles Rodger and Margaret Tait, born 7 Aug. bapt. 19 Nov. 1815. [S]

ROGER, HANNAH, a spinster in Dundee, married Abraham Campbell, a bachelor in Dundee, in the vestry of the Scots Episcopal Chapel in Dundee on 21 Oct. 1821. [S]

RODGER, HENRY JOHN, son of Richard Rodger and his wife Elizabeth, born 16 Jan., bapt. 9 Feb. 1817. [S]

RODGER, JANET JANE, born 21 Feb. bapt. 14 Mar. 1819, 3rd dau. of Richard Chalmers Rodger, a writer [lawyer] born in Dundee, and his wife Elizabeth, dau. of John Anderson a farmer in Upper Clochan, Raffin, Banffshire. [E]

RODGER, THOMAS, pensioner, 1745. [DCA.GD/EC/D10/2/1]

RODGER, THOMAS, son of Richard C. Rodger and his wife Betsey, born 31 Oct. bapt. 26 Nov. 1812. [S]

ROGERS, ALFRED HORATIO, 2nd son of John Henry Rogers, organist, born in Leeds, Yorkshire, England, and his wife Caroline, dau. of John Cliff, a merchant in Swallow Street, London, born 14 Nov. bapt. 30 Dec. 1810. [E]

ROGERS, EUPHEMIA, dau. of William Rogers and his wife Susan, born 23 Mar., bapt. 7 Apl. 1816. [S]

ROGERS, JAMES MUIR, son of John Henry Rogers and Caroline his wife, born 24 Feb. bapt. 8 Apr. 1815. [S]

ROGERS, JOHN H., organist, 1816/1817. [S][DCA.GD.EC.D10.1/2]

ROHELDER, JOHN, member of the QEC, 1776. [DCA:GD/EC/D10/1/1]

ROLLO, Mrs, a widow, pensioner, 1739. [DCA.GD/EC/DIO/2/1]

ROSIN, HANNAH VAN LOON, 1st dau of Peter Rosin, sailor, born in Amsterdam, the Netherlands, and his wife Margaret, dau. of Thomas Kerr, a brewer in Dundee, born 22 Dec. bapt. 29 Dec. 1811. [E]

ROSIN, DAVID HOWIE, born 10 Sep. 1817, 2nd son of Peter Rosin, a sailor, born in Amsterdam, the Netherlands, and his wife Margaret, dau. of Thomas Kerr, a brewer in Dundee. [E]

ROSIN, JANE BRECHIN, born 7 Sep., bapt. 12 Sept. 1819, 2nd son of Peter Rosin, a sailor, born in Amsterdam, the Netherlands, and his wife Margaret, dau. of Thomas Kerr, a brewer in Dundee. [E]

ROSIN, THOMAS KERR, 1st son of Peter Rosin, sailor, born in Amsterdam, the Netherlands, and his wife Margaret, dau. of Thomas Kerr, a brewer in Dundee, born 19 May, bapt. 22 May 1811. [E]

ROSS, CHRISTOPHER, 1784. [DCA.GD/EC/D10/2/2][E]

ROSS, DANIEL, a bachelor in Dundee, and Margaret Nicoll, a spinster in Dundee, were married in the house of Thomas Nicoll, Hawkhill Place, Dundee,9 June 1828. [S]

ROSS, JENNY, dau of William Ross and Ellen his wife, born 28 Apr. bapt. 31 May 1814. [S]

ROSS, MARY, dau. of Alexander Ross and Margaret his wife, born 9 Mar. bapt. 16 Apr. 1815. [S]

ROUGH, THOMAS, member of the QEC, 1776. [DCA:GD/EC/D10/1/1]

RUSSEL, MARIA, born 28 Sep.1828, bapT. 13 May 1829, 4th dau. of John Russel, a weaver, born in Newry, County Down, Ireland, and his wife Margaret, dau. of David Wright, a weaver in Newry, County Down. [E]

RUSSEL, WILLIAM PEDDY, 1st son of William Russel, a Private of the 25th Regiment of Foot, born in Dundee, and his wife Agnes, dau. of Andrew Gregg, a ships-carpenter in Dundee, born 15 Sept. bapt. 1 Oct. 1809. [E]

RUSSELL, ..., church member, 1758. [DCA.GD/EC/D10/2/2][E]

RYMER, WILLIAM, in Dundee, and Mary Mudie in Dundee, were married the house of Rev. John Hetherton, Paton's Lane, Dundee, 28 Nov 1831. [S]

SADDLER, ALEXANDER, member of the QEC, 1776. [DCA:GD/EC/D10/1/1]

SADDLER, ALLAN, beadle, 1781. [DCA.GD/EC/D10/2/2][E]

SADDLER, GEORGE OGILVIE, vestryman of the QEC, 1783 [DCA:GD/EC/D10/1/1]

SALMON, ELIZABETH STEWART, born 5 Mar., bapt. 25 Mar. 1821, dau. of Elizabeth Stewart, dau. of the late Daniel Stewart a weaver in Wick, Caithness. [E]

SAMSON, HUGH, a bachelor in Dundee, and Margaret Watson, a spinster in Dundee, were married in the vestry of St Paul's, Castle Street, Dundee, 28 Mar. 1829. [S]

SAMSON, JAMES, son of George Samson and Margaret Murray born 16 Nov 1815, bapt. 10 Mar. 1816. [S]

SAMPSON, Miss, member of the QEC, 1776. [DCA:GD/EC/D10/1/1]

SANDIEMAN, CHARLES, a pensioner aged 68 in 1818. [S] [DCA.GD.EC.D10.1/2]

SANDIEMAN, DAVID, son of Charles Sandieman and Elizabeth, his wife, born 4 Jan., bapT. 5 Jan. 1817. [S]

SANDIEMAN, JOHN, vestryman, 1802. [DCA.GD/EC/D10/1/2][S]

SANDIEMAN, JOHN, son of Charles Sandieman and his wife Elizabeth born 17 Aug. bapt. 18 Aug 1811. [S]

SANDIEMAN, the Misses, church members, 1810. [DCA.GD/EC/D10/1/2][S]

SAUNDERS, MARTHA, dau. of Henry Saunders and his wife Janet, born 6 Jan., bapt. 9 Jan. 1817. [S]

SAUNDERS, PATERSON, a writer, [lawyer], church member, 1810. [DCA.GD/EC/D10/1/2][S]

SANDERS, PATTERSON, infant son of Patterson Sanders, Writer to the Signet, Tay Street, Dundee, born 1806, died 19 Nov. 1808. [E]

SAVAGE, ANDREW, born 24 July bapt. 17 Aug. 1828, 3rd son of Samuel Savage, a flax dresser, born Comber, County Down, Ireland,

and his wife Susanna, daughter of the late Anthony Hamil, a weaver in Ramsden, County Antrim, Ireland. [E]

SAVAGE, MARGARET, born 28 April, bapt. 2 May 1824, 3rd dau of Samuel Savage, a flax dresser, born Comber, County Down, Ireland, and his wife Susanna, daughter of the late Anthony Hamil, a weaver in Ramsden, County Antrim, Ireland. [E]

SAVAGE, RICHARD, born 11 Oct. bapt. 13 Oct. 1822, 3RD son of Samuel Savage, a flax dresser, born Comber, County Down, Ireland, and his wife Susanna, daughter of the late Anthony Hamil, a weaver in Ramsden, County Antrim, Ireland. [E]

SAVAGE, ROSANNA, born 19 Sep. bapt. 25 Sep. 1825, 3rd dau of Samuel Savage, a flax dresser, born Comber, County Down, Ireland, and his wife Susanna, daughter of the late Anthony Hamil, a weaver in Ramsden, County Antrim, Ireland. [E]

SCOLIN, ANDREW, a bachelor in Dundee, and Ann Dollard, a spinster in Dundee, were married in the vestry of St Paul's, Castle Street, Dundee, 18 Feb. 1831. [S]

SCOTT, AGNES, dau. of John Scott and Isabel his wife, born 14 Sep. bapt. 16 Oct. 1814. [S]

SCOTT, ALEXANDER, son of James Scott and Agnes Laurence, born 9 July, bapt. 31 July 1814. [S]

SCOTT, CHARLES, son of William Scott and Janet Blair, born 22 Dec. 1814, bapt. 1 Jan. 1815. [S]

SCOTT, DAVID, a merchant in Dundee, vestryman of the QEC, a manager, 1757; 1764; 1768; 1771; 1776. [DCA:GD/EC/D10/1/1; 2/2] [DCA.RD29.866]

SCOTT, DAVID, a weaver, church member, 1777. [DCA:GD/EC/D10/1/2][S]

SCOTT, DAVID, a merchant, church member, 1784. [DCA.GD/EC/D10/2/2][E]

SCOTT, DAVID, son of William Scott and Elizabeth Cudbert, born 7 May, bapt. 18 June 1815. [S]

SCOTT, DAVID, son of David Scott and Anne Anderson, born 4 June, bapt. 11 June 1815. [S]

SCOTT, ELIZABETH, a spinster in Dundee, and James Latto, a bachelor in Dundee, were married in the vestry of St Paul's, Castle Street, Dundee, 14 May 1829. [S]

SCOTT, FREDERICK, son of Frederick Scott and Christian Archibald, born 5 Feb. bapt. 23 Feb. 1812. [S]

SCOTT, GEORGE, a gentleman's servant, and Helen Miller, both in Dundee, were married 31 Dec. 1820. [E]

SCOTT, GRIZEL, widow of Lewis Hay the Supervisor of Excise in Dundee, deceased by 1783. [DCA:GD/EC/D10/1/1]

SCOTT, JOHN, a brewer, church member, 1777. [DCA.GD/EC/D10/1/2][S]

SCOTT, JOHN, vestryman, 1819. [S][DCA.GD.EC.D10.1/2]

SCOTT, Mrs JOHN, a member of the Scots Episcopal Chapel, Castle Street, Dundee, 1824. [DCA.GD.EC.D10.1/3]

SCOTT, MARY ANNE, dau. of James Scott and Jane Ogilvie, born 9 Dec. 1812, bapt. 31 Jan. 1813. [S]

SCOTT, SUSAN, among the 'poor of St Paul's 1830' [DCA.GD.EC.D10.1/3]

SCOTT, THOMAS, a widower in Dundee, and Mary Boyd, a widow in Dundee, were married in the house of Rev. H. Horseley, Magdalene Yard, Perth Road, Dundee, 30 Oct. 1836. [S]

SCOTT, WILLIAM, church member, 1764. [DCA.GD/EC/DIO/2/1]

SCOTT, WILLIAM, a silversmith, vestryman of the English Chapel in Dundee, 1783, 1784, 1808. [DCA:GD/EC/D10/1/1][E] [DCA.GD/EC/D10/2/2]

SCOTT, WILLIAM, son of James Scott and Margaret his wife, born 1 May, bapt. 31 May 1814. [S]

SCOTT, Sir WILLIAM, of Ancrum, Roxburghshire, a bachelor, and Elizabeth Anderson, a spinster in Dundee, were married in the house of Mrs Anderson, Balgay, Angus, 9 June 1828. [S]

SCRIMGURE, JOHN, son of John Scrimgure and Elizabeth Adams, bapt. 18 Aug. 1811. [S]

SHAND, HELEN CLARK, born 17 Sep., bapt. 8 Oct. 1826, 2nd dau. of William Shand, a shoemaker, born in Aberdeen, and his wife Anne, dau. of William Ross a labourer in Dundee. [E]

SEAMAN, JOHANNA, dau. of John Seaman and Christian Mackay born 24 Dec. 1813, bapt. 16 Jan. 1814. [S]

SEWELL, ..., minister of the Qualified Chapel in Dundee, from 1749 until 1750. [DCA.GD/EC/D10/2/2][E]

SHAW, BETTY, dau. of James Shaw and Amelia Jakes, born 20 June, bapt. 4 July 1813. [S]

SHAW, JANE, born 3 Oct., bapt. 19 Oct. 1823, 1st dau. of David Shaw, a weaver, born in Dundee, and his wife Mary, dau. of John Kelly, a slater in Liverpool, England. [E]

SHEIN, MARGARET, pensioner, 1740. [DCA.GD/EC/DIO/2/1]

SHELDON, EMMA CROSBY, born 5 Nov. 1819, bapt. 3 Feb. 1820, first dau. of John Sheldon, born in Sheffield, Yorkshire, England, a Sergeant of the 4th Royal Veteran Battalion, and his wife Bridget, dau. of Owen Crosby, a farmer in Roscommon, Ireland. [E]

SIDEY, ELIZABETH, born 10 Sep. bapt. 8 Oct. 1820, 2nd dau. of John Sidey, a seaman born in Dundee, and his wife Elizabeth, dau. of David Watson a cutler in Dundee. [E]

SIDEY, JOHN CHRISTIE WILKIE, born 20 Sep. bapt. 29 Oct.1820, son of Margaret Sidey, dau. of Alexander Sidey, a porter in Dundee. [E]

SIDEY, MARGARET, born 24 Dec. bapt. 23 Jan. 1829, 4th dau. of John Sidey, a seaman born in Dundee, and his wife Elizabeth, dau. of David Watson a cutler in Dundee. [E]

SIEVEWRIGHT, JOHN, a tailor, church member, 1777. [DCA:GD/EC/D10/1/2][S]

SIM, ISABEL, dau. of David Sim and Anne Bankes, born 14 Apr. bapt. 24 July 1814. [S]

SIME, THOMAS, a merchant, QEC vestryman, 1769; 1776. [DCA:GD/EC/D10/1/1]

SIME, Mrs, member of the QEC, 1776. [DCA:GD/EC/D10/1/1]

SIMSON, ALEXANDER, member of the QEC, 1776, [DCA:GD/EC/D10/1/1]

SIMPSON, EUPHEMIA, dau. of Alexander Simpson and Elspeth Cowdie, born 2 Apr. bapt. 4 July 1813. [S]

SIMPSON, Mrs, pensioner, 1739. [DCA.GD/EC/DIO/2/1]

SIMPSON, AGNES WYLIE, born 25 Jan., bapt. 6 Mar. 1829, 4th dau. of Robert Simpson, master mariner of the sloop Mary, born in Longforgan, Perthshire and his wife Janet, dau. of James Buchan a shoemaker in Glasgow. [E]

SIMPSON, Miss ELIZABETH, a member of the Scots Episcopal Chapel, Castle Street, Dundee, 1824. [DCA.GD.EC.D10.1/3]

SIMPSON, GEORGE BUCHAN, born 19 Sep. bapt. 10 Oct. 1820, third son of Robert Simpson, master mariner of the sloop Mary, born in Longforgan, Perthshire, and his wife Janet, dau. of James Buchan a shoemaker in Glasgow. [E]

SIMPSON, JANE, born 18 July, bapt. 8 Aug.1826, dau. of Robert Simpson, master mariner of the sloop Mary, born in Longforgan, Perthshire, and his wife Janet, dau. of James Buchan, a shoemaker in Glasgow. [E]

SIMPSON, JANET, born 16 Dec. bapt. 5 Jan. 1817, dau. of Robert Simpson, master mariner of the sloop Mary, born in Longforgan, Perthshire, and his wife Janet, dau. of James Buchan, a shoemaker in Glasgow. [E]

SIMPSON, MARGARET CUTHBERT, born 5 June, bapt. 25 June 1823, 2ND dau. of Robert Simpson, master mariner of the sloop Mary, born in Longforgan, Perthshire, and his wife Janet, dau. of James Buchan, a shoemaker in Glasgow. [E]

SIMPSON, ROBERT, born 4 Dec. bapt. 18 Dec. 1818, 1st son of Robert Simpson, master mariner of the sloop Mary, born in Longforgan, Perthshire, and his wife Janet, dau. of James Buchan, a shoemaker in Glasgow. [E]

SIVEWRIGHT, F., clerk, 1756. [DCA.GD/EC/D10/2/2][E]

SKEETS, Reverend HENRY ATWOOD, MA, minister of the English Chapel in Perth, and Elizabeth, dau. of Dr John Lewis in Perth, were married 19 Oct. 1812. [E]

SKENE, PATRICK GEORGE, in Strathmiglo, Fife, and Emily Rait in Dundee, were married at Craigie, Angus, 25 Aug. 1826. [E]

SKIRLING, DAVID, church member, 1743. [DCA.GD/EC/D10/2/3]

SKIRLING, JOHN, church member, 1743. [DCA.GD/EC/DIO/2/1; 2/3]

SKIRLING, PATRICK or PETER, a brewer, church member, 1743, 1746. [DCA.GD/EC/DIO/2/1]

SKIRLING, WILLIAM, a brewer, QEC vestryman, 1769. [DCA:GD/EC/D10/1/1]

SLIDER, ANNE, dau of William Slider and Rachel Robert, born 18 Aug. bapt. 13 Sept. 1812. [S]

SMALL, ANDREW, in Dundee, and Elizabeth Robertson, in Dundee, were married in the house of John Robertson, Horsewater Wynd, Dundee, 5 Apl. 1832. [S]

SMALL, DAVID MACPHERSON, son of Thomas Small and Elizabeth his wife, born 13 Dec. bapt. 27 Dec. 1815. [S]

SMALL, MARGARET, dau. of William Small and Charlotte his wife, born 20 Sept. bapt. 9 Nov. 1813. [S]

SMALL, WILLIAM, son of William Small and Charlotte his wife, born 2 Mar., bapt. 23 Mar. 1815. [S]

SMALL, WILLIAM, a vestryman,1814/1816/1819. [S][DCA.GD.EC.D10.1/2]

SMART, BETTY, dau. of David Smart and Ellen Stuart, born 1 Feb, bapt. 17 Mar. 1813. [S]

SMART, CATHERINE, pensioner, 1745. [DCA.GD/EC/D10/2/1]

SMART, CHRISTY, dau. of David Smart and Christy Scrimgure, born 27 Oct. 1811, bapt. 14 Mar 1812. [S]

SMART, ELIZA, 2nd dau of William Smart a weaver, born in Arbroath, Angus, and his wife Margaret, dau. of John Higgins labourer, born in Ballyhinch, County Cork, Ireland, born 19 July, bapt. 9 Aug. 1812. [E]

SMART, JOHN MITCHELL, son of David Smart and Margaret his wife, bapt. 2 Feb. 1812. [S]

SMART, MARIA, 1st dau of William Smart a weaver, born in Arbroath, Angus, and his wife Margaret, dau. of John Higgins labourer, born in Ballyhinch, County Cork, Ireland, born 23 June, bapt. 2 July 1809. [E]

SMART, THOMAS, church member, 1764. [DCA.GD/EC/DIO/2/1]

SMITH, ALEXANDER, and his wife, members of the Scots Episcopal Chapel, Castle Street, Dundee, 1824. [DCA.GD.EC.D10.1/3]

SMITH, ANDREW, a smith, church member, 1777. [DCA:GD/EC/D10/1/2][S]

SMITH, ANDREW, QEC church member, 1811. [DCA:GD/EC/D10/1/1]

SMITH, ANDREW, son of Andrew Smith and Anne Smith, born 12 Sept, bapt. 12 Nov. 1815. [S]

SMITH, ANN, 2nd dau of John Smith, a mariner, born in Danzig, Prussia, and his wife Isabella, dau. of James Henderson, a slater in Dundee, born 11 June, bapt. 12 June 1814. [E]

SMITH, ANN, born 4 Nov., bapt. 7 Dec. 1823, 3rd dau. of Henry Smith, a professor of music and church organist, born in St Mary's, Whitechapel, London, and his wife Dorothy Mary, dau. of George Snuggs, coach-maker in St Olave's, Rotherhithe, London. [E]

SMITH, ANNY, dau. of Robert Smith and Anny Douglas, born Aug. bapt. 18 Sept. 1811. [S]

SMITH, CHARLES, son of John Smith and Anne his wife, born 19 May bapt. 11 June 1815. [S]

SMITH, DOROTHY MARY, born 26 Nov., bapt. 19 Dec. 1824, dau. of Henry Smith, a professor of music and church organist, born in St Mary's, Whitechapel, London, and his wife Dorothy Mary, dau. of George Snuggs, coach-maker in St Olave's, Rotherhithe, London. [E]

SMITH, EDWARD, 8th son of Henry Smith a nailer, born in Dundee, and his wife Helen, dau of John Jones, a tallow chandler in Coot Hill, County Cavan, Ireland, born 23 July, bapt. 7 Aug. 1814. [E]

SMITH, EDWARD, born 2 Oct., bap. 7 Dec. 1818, son of Henry Smith, a professor of music and church organist, born in St Mary's, Whitechapel, London, and his wife Dorothy Mary, dau. of George Snuggs, coach-maker in St Olave's, Rotherhithe, London. [E]

SMITH, ELIZABETH, dau. of John Smith and Isabell Henderson his wife, born 27 Aug. bapt. 17 Sept. 1811. [S]

SMITH, ELIZABETH, born 21 Oct., bapt. 3 Nov. 1816, dau. of Henry Smith, a nailer, born in Dundee, and his wife Helen Jones, dau. of John Jones, a tallow chandler of Coast Hill, County Cavan, Ireland. [E]

SMITH, ELSPET, pensioner, 1740. [DCA.GD/EC/DIO/2/1]

SMITH, JAMES, weaver, church member, 1777. [DCA.GD/EC/D10/1/2][S]

SMITH, JAMES, QEC church member, 1811. [DCA:GD/EC/D10/1/1]

SMITH, JAMES, son of Peter Smith and Janet Sinclair, born 23 Apr. bapt. 16 May 1813. [S]

SMITH, JAMES, son of James Smith and Ellen his wife, born 26 Apl., bapt. 12 May 1816. [S]

SMITH, JAMES, and his wife, members of the Scots Episcopal Chapel, Castle Street, Dundee, 1824. [DCA.GD.EC.D10.1/3]

SMITH, JANE, dau. of George Smith and Agnes his wife, born 30 Jan bapt. 7 May 1815. [S]

SMITH, JANET, 2nd dau. of Henry Smith, a nailer, born in Dundee, and his wife Helen, dau. of John Jones, a tallow chandler in Coot Hill, County Cavan, Ireland, born 24 May, bapt. 7 June 1812. [E]

SMITH, JEAN, pensioner, 1740. [DCA.GD/EC/DIO/2/1]

SMITH, JOHN, (1), member QEC, 1776; day labourer, 1777. [DCA:GD/EC/D10/1/1,2]

SMITH, JOHN, (2), member QEC, 1776. [DCA:GD/EC/D10/1/1]

SMITH, JOHN, 1st son of George Smith, farmer of Bogside, Tannadice, Angus, born there, and his wife Agnes, dau. of William Candy, farmer of Newbiggin, Angus, born in Cortachy, Angus, born 21 Feb. bapt. 8 Apr. 1809. [E]

SMITH, JOHN, son of Thomas Smith and Elizabeth his wife, born 1 Sept. bapt. 24 Sept. 1815. [S]

SMITH, JOHN, born 15 May, bapt. 18 May 1817 18 May 1817, son of John Smith, a mariner born in Danzig, [Gdansk], Prussia, and his wife Isabella, dau. of James Henderson, a slater in Dundee. [E]

SMITH, JOHN ARBUTHNOTT, born 27 July, bapt. 2 Aug 1822, 3rd son of Henry Smith, a professor of music and church organist, born in St Mary's, Whitechapel, London, and his wife Dorothy Mary, dau. of George Snuggs, a coach-maker in St Olave's, Rotherhithe, London. [E]

SMITH, Miss J., a member of the Scots Episcopal Chapel, Castle Street, Dundee, 1824. [DCA.GD.EC.D10.1/3]

SMITH, LOUISE WETHERTON, born 10 Jan. bapt. 6 Feb. 1820, 2nd dau. of Henry Smith, a professor of music and church organist, born in St Mary's, Whitechapel, London, and his wife Dorothy Mary, dau. of George Snuggs, a coach-maker in St Olave's, Rotherhithe, London. [E]

SMITH, LOUISE WETHERTON, born 29 Mar. bapt. 23 Apr. 1826, 5th dau. of Henry Smith, a professor of music and church organist, born in St Mary's, Whitechapel, London, and his wife Dorothy Mary, dau. of George Snuggs, a coach-maker in St Olave's, Rotherhithe, London. [E]

SMITH, MARGARET, pensioner, 1743. [DCA.GD/EC/D10/2/1]

SMITH, MARGARET, born 7 Feb., bapt. 20 Feb. 1820, dau. of Henry Smith, a nailer, born in Dundee, and his wife Helen Jones, dau. of John Jones, a tallow chandler of Coast Hill, County Cavan, Ireland. [E]

SMITH, PETER, son of John Robertson Smith and Elizabeth Guild, born 10 Sept, bapt. 11 Dec 1814. [S]

SMITH, PETER, son of Peter Smith and Elizabeth Grant, born 21 Aug 1815, bapt. 12 Apr. 1816. [S]

SMITH, ROBERT, son of David Smith and his wife Margaret, born 29 Sep. bapt. 13 Oct. 1816. [S]

SMITH, SALLY, dau. of James Smith and his wife Ellen, bapt. 5 Mar. 1811. [S]

SMITH, WILLIAM, 3rd son of George Smith farmer of Bogside, Tannadice, Angus, and his wife Agnes, dau. of William Candy, in Newbiggin, Cortachy Angus, born 18 Sep, bapt. 7 Oct. 1810. [E]

SMITH, WILLIAM, 1st son of John Smith, a mariner, born in Danzig, Prussia, Germany, and his wife Isabella, dau. of James Henderson, a slater in Dundee, born 4 Nov, bapt 19 Nov 1815. [E]

SMITH, WILLIAM, a labourer in Leuchars, Fife, a bachelor, married Catherine Mill, a spinster in Leuchars, at the house of Mrs Addison, High Street, Dundee, 9 May 1819. [S]

SMITHFIELD, Lady, church member 1746, 1750. [DCA.GD/EC/D10/2/1]

SNELL, EDWARD KEATS NELSON, born 6 Oct., bapt. 21 Oct. 1823, 2nd son of Robert Snell, Lieutenant of the Royal Navy, born in Chawleigh, Devon, England, and his wife Betsey, dau. of Alexander Black, master in the Royal Navy, lately resident in Hoo, Kent, England. [E]

SNELL, ELIZABETH MARY, born 7 July, bapt. 27 Aug. 1817, dau. of Robert Snell, Lieutenant of the Royal Navy, born in Chawleigh, Devon, England, and his wife Betsey, dau. of Alexander Black, master in the Royal Navy, lately resident in Hoo, Kent, England. [E]

SNELL, WILLIAM BLACK, born 6 Aug, bapt. 7 Oct. 1818, son of Robert Snell, Lieutenant of the Royal Navy, born in Chawleigh, Devon, England, and his wife Betsey, dau. of Alexander Black, master in the Royal Navy, lately resident in Hoo, Kent, England. [E]

SNODGRASS, JANET, born 4 Sept, bapt. 5 Oct. 1823, 2nd dau of John Snodgrass, a travelling mason, born in Edinburgh, and his wife Mary, dau. of William McMillan, a blacksmith in Glasgow. [E]

SOOT, JAMES, a widower in Dundee, and Agnes Speid, a widow in Dundee, were married in the house of Agnes Speid, Wellgait, Dundee, 25 Nov. 1830. [S]

SOUTAR, JOHN, a shoemaker, church member, 1777, 1781. [DCA:GD/EC/D10/1/2][S]

SOUTAR, ROBERT, son of Robert Soutar, a tailor in Dundee, bapt. 27 July 1725. [BN]

SPANKIE, THOMAS, son of James Spankie and Janet his wife, born 18 July, bapt. 2 Aug 1812. [S]

SPARKS, ANN, a spinster in Dundee, and George Lowrie, a bachelor in Dundee, were married in the vestry of St Paul's, Castle Street, Dundee, 28 Oct. 1827. [S]

SPARKES, DAVID, son of John Sparkes and Susan his wife, born 22 July, bapt. 4 Aug. 1812. [S]

SPEID, JAMES, member of the QEC, 1776. [DCA:GD/EC/D10/1/1]

SPEID, ROBERT, a merchant in Dundee, vestryman of the QEC, a manager, 1757; 1764, 1768, 1771. [DCA:GD/EC/D10/1/1; 2/2][E] [DCA.RD29.866]

SPEID, THOMAS, shoemaker, vestryman of the QEC, 1758, 1764; 1776. [DCA:GD/EC/D10/1/1] [DCA.GD/EC/D10/2/2][E]

SPEID, Mrs, member QEC, 1776. [DCA:GD/EC/D10/1/1]

STANNERS, DAVID, church officer, 1740. [DCA.GD/EC/DIO/2/1]

STEELE, CATHERINE, a spinster in St Cuthbert's parish, Edinburgh, and James Stewart Ducat, a Writer to the Signet, parish of St Stephen, Edinburgh, married in the house of Mrs George Greig, Tay Square, Dundee, 9 Sept.1834. [S]

STEEL, ELLEN MILLAR, dau. of Peter Steel and Margaret Morren, born 2 Apr. bapt. 9 Oct. 1814. [S]

STEEL, JAMES, born 8 June, bapt. 20 July 1828, 5th son of Adam Steel, a labourer, born in St Quivox, Ayrshire, and his wife Elizabeth, dau. of Robert MacCartell a labourer in St Quivox. [E]

STEPHEN, EBENEZER, a mason in Dundee, a bachelor, married Euphemia Beattie, a spinster in Dundee, at the house of Andrew Hood, a vintner in St Clement's Lane, Dundee, on 9 May 1819. [S]

STEPHENS, ELIZABETH, 4th dau. of Robert Stephens, pilot of HMS Cherokee, born in Monifieth, Angus, and his wife Mary, dau. of Thomas Brewer, a labourer in Offington, Exeter, Devon, England, born 25 Sept. bapt. 4 Oct. 1812. [E]

STEVEN, JOHN, goldsmith, vestryman of the QEC, 1757; 1764. [DCA:GD/EC/D10/1/1] [DCA.GD/EC/D10/2/2][E]

STEPHEN, WILLIAM, a writer, [lawyer], in Dundee, a bachelor, and Margaret Inglis, a spinster in Dundee, were married in the house of Mrs Inglis, Nethergait, Dundee, 9 Feb. 1835. [S]

STEVEN, Miss, member of the QEC, 1776. [DCA:GD/EC/D10/1/1]

STEVENSON, JANET, born 27 Dec. 1820, bapt. 14 Jan. 1821, 2nd dau. of James Stevenson, a mason born in Brechin, Angus, and his wife Margaret, dau. of Robert Hill a shoemaker in Dundee. [E]

STEVENSON, JEAN, pensioner, 1739. [DCA.GD/EC/DIO/2/1]

STEVENSON, JOHN, born 20 Dec. bapt. 5 Jan 1817, son of James Stevenson, a mason born in Brechin, Angus, and his wife Margaret, dau. of Robert Hill, a shoemaker in Dundee. [E]

STEVENSON, MARGARET, born 4 Mar. bapt. 8 Mar. 1819, son of James Stevenson, a mason born in Brechin, Angus, and his wife Margaret, dau. of Robert Hill, a shoemaker in Dundee. [E]

STEWART, ADAM, 3rd son of Rigg Stewart, a Private of the 42nd Regiment of Foot, born in Cupar, Fife, and his wife Mary, dau. of William Mills weaver in Kirriemuir, Angus, born 4 March, bapt. 31 May 1810. [E]

STEWART, ALEXANDER, church member, 1743. [DCA.GD/EC/DIO/2/1; 2/3]; pensioner, 1745. [DCA.GD/EC/D10/2/1] [a Jacobite in 1745]

STEWART, ANN, 6th dau. of Robert Stewart, a weaver, born in Stonehaven, Kincardineshire, and his wife Ann, dau of William Jolly a labourer in Montrose, Angus, born 25 July, bapt. 2 Aug 1812. [E]

STEWART, CHARLES, church member, 1781. [DCA.GD/EC/D10/1/2][S]

STEWART, Sir GEORGE, of Grandtully, Perthshire, vestryman of the QEC, 1757. [DCA:GD/EC/D10/1/1] [DCA.GD/EC/D10/2/2][E]

STEWART, JAMES, died 1760. [DCA.GD/EC/D10/2/2][E]

STEWART, JAMES, church member, 1781. [DCA.GD/EC/D10/1/2][S]

STEWART, JAMES HACKNEY, 5th son of Robert Stewart weaver, born in Stonehaven, Kincardineshire, and his wife Ann, dau. of William Jolly a labourer in Montrose, Angus, born 27 Jan. bapt. 3 Feb. 1811. [E]

STEWART, JOHN, church member, 1781. [DCA.GD/EC/D10/1/2][S]

STEWART, JOHN, of the Scots Episcopal Chapel, Castle Street, Dundee, 1824. [DCA.GD.EC.D0.1/3]

STEWART, PETER, a shoemaker, and Agnes Adam, both in Dundee, were married on 21 Mar. 1820. [E]

STEWART, ROBERT, a surgeon, church member, 1784, 1799. [DCA.GD/EC/D10/2/2][E]

STEWART, Lady, church member, 1758. [DCA.GD/EC/D10/2/2][E]

STEWART, WILLIAM, church member, 1764. [DCA.GD/EC/DIO/2/1]

STEWART, ..., church member, 1764. [DCA.GD/EC/DIO/2/1]

NOTE: These two entries were added later by the author. No further text belongs on this page.

STEWART, Miss, a vestryman, St Paul's, Dundee, 1835.
[DCA.GD.EC.D10.1-3]

STIRLING, CHARLES, a bachelor from Cadder, Lanarkshire, married Christian Erskine, spinster in Monifieth, Angus, at the house of Thomas Erskine, Linlathen, Angus, 14 Oct. 1817. [S]

STIRLING, JAMES, church member, 1781. [DCA.GD/EC/D10/1/2][S]

STIRLING, PATRICK, a merchant, church member, 1784.
[DCA.GD/EC/D10/2/2][E]

STIRLING, Captain ROBERT, QEC vestryman, 1764. [DCA:GD/EC/D10/1/1]
[DCA.GD/EC/D10/2/2][E]

STIRLING, ROBERT, a merchant, vestryman of the QEC, 1810.
[DCA.GD/EC/D10/1/2]

STIRLING, ROBERT, a merchant in Dundee, 1825; vestryman, St Paul's, Dundee, 1830/1835. [DCA.GD.EC.D10.1/3]

STIRLING, Miss, member of the QEC, 1776. [DCA:GD/EC/D10/1/1]

STIVENSON, ALEXANDER, a wright, church member, 1777.
[DCA:GD/EC/D10/1/2][S]

STOBBIE, ALEXANDER, born 9 Feb. bapt. 24 Feb. 1819, 2nd son of Alexander Stobbie, a mariner, born in Dundee, and his wife Elizabeth, dau. of Thomas Carr, a brewer in Dundee, born 19 July, bapt. 6 Aug. 1815. [E]

STOBBIE, JAMES, born 22 Mar. bapt. 29 Mar. 1822, 3rd son of Alexander, son of Alexander Stobbie, a mariner, born in Dundee, and his wife Elizabeth, dau. of Thomas Carr, a brewer in Dundee, born 19 July, bapt. 6 Aug. 1815. [E]

STOBBIE, WILLIAM, born 19 July, bapt.6 Aug. 1815, 1st son of Alexander Stobbie, a mariner, born in Dundee, and his wife Elizabeth, dau. of Thomas Carr, a brewer in Dundee. [E]

STORMONTH, ALEXANDER, a bachelor, and Elizabeth Stewart, a spinster, both in Dundee, were married on 24 Jan. 1814, witnesses were Elizabeth and Isabella Stormonth. [S]

STORMONTH, Dr ALEXANDER, a vestryman, 1816/1818/1819/1820.
[S][DCA.GD.EC.D10.1/2]

STORMONTH, CATHERINE, dau. of Alexander Stormonth and Elizabeth his wife, born 1 Nov. bapt. 4 Dec. 1814. [S]

STORMONTH, JAMES, son of Alexander Stormonth and Elizabeth his wife, born 30 May, bapt. 23 June 1816. [S]

STRACHAN, ALEXANDER, a merchant in Dundee, QEC committee, 1757; vestryman, manager, 1764, 1768; 1771; 1776, 1784.
[DCA:GD/EC/D10/1/1; 2/2] [DCA.RD29.866][E]

STRACHAN, ANNE, dau. of Alexander Strachan and Margaret his wife, born 3 Feb. bapt. 2 Apr. 1815. [S]

STRACHAN, Captain JAMES, QEC committee, 1757
[DCA:GD/EC/D10/1/1] [DCA.GD/EC/D10/2/2][E]

STRACHAN, JOHN, a merchant in Dundee, QEC committee, 1757.
[DCA:GD/EC/D10/1/1] [DCA.GD/EC/D10/2/2][E]

STRACHAN, JOHN, of St Paul's, Dundee, from 1780 until 1810.
[Dundee Directory, 1782, etc] [DCA.GD/EC/D10/1/2]

STUART, ALLEN, son of Sanders Stuart and Janet Butchart, born 4 May 1811, bapt. 9 Apr. 1813. [S]

STUART, JOHN ALEXANDER, son of John Stuart, a Sergeant of the 2nd Battalion of the 79th Regiment of Foot, and Esther his wife, born 22 Sept. bapt. 10 Oct. 1813. [S]

STUART, ROBERT, son of George Stuart and Margaret his wife, born 20 Apr. bapt. 7 May 1815. [S]

STUART, ROBERT, son of John Stuart and Esther his wife, born 28 Aug, bapt. 17 Sept 1815. [S]

STUART, WILLIAM, a slater, church member, 1777.
[DCA.GD/EC/D10/1/2][S]

STURRETT, CHARLES, born 3 June, bapt. 21 June, 182-, 1st son of David Sturrett, a shoemaker, born in Raphoe, County Donegal, Ireland, and his wife Mary, dau. of James Holmes a farmer in Niverny, Donoughmore, County Donegal, Ireland. [E]

STURROCK, ARCHIBALD, son of John Sturrock and Christine his wife, born 30 Sep., bapt. 20 Oct. 1816. [S]

STURROCK, DAVID, a weaver, church member, 1810.
[DCA.GD/EC/D10/1/2][S]

STURROCK, DAVID, 2nd son of David Sturrock, baker, born in Monikie Angus, and his wife Hesther, dau. of Robert Conyers a poulterer in Westminster, London, born 24 Dec. bapt. 29 Dec. 1811. [E]

STURROCK, DAVID, a member of the Scots Episcopal Chapel, Castle Street, Dundee, 1824. [DCA.GD.EC.D10.1/3]

STURROCK, HESTER, 4th dau. of David Sturrock, baker, born in Monikie, Angus, and his wife Hesther, dau. of Robert Conyers a poulterer in Westminster, London, born 25 Aug. bapt. 5 Sep. 1813. [E]

STURROCK, JAMES, son of Thomas Sturrock and his wife Lanceman, born 25 July, bapt. 18 Aug. 1811. [S]

STURROCK, JOHN, a merchant, church treasurer, 1810.
[DCA.GD/EC/D10/1/2] [S] a vestryman/treasurer, 1816/1817/1818/ 1819/1820/1825/1828/1830; a member of the Scots Episcopal Church, Castle Street, Dundee.

STURROCK, MARY, dau. of David Sturrock, a baker, born in Monikie, Angus, and his wife Hesther, dau. of Robert Conyers, a poulterer in Westminster, London, born 24 Jan. bapt. 4 Feb. 1810. [E]

STURROCK, MARY, dau. of David Sturrock and Jane his wife, born 20 Jan. bapt. 30 Jan. 1814. [S]

STURROCK, ROBERT, son of John Sturrock and Christian his wife, born 6 July, bapt. 8 Aug. 1815. [S]

STURROCK, ROBERT, 4th son of David Sturrock, a baker, born in Monikie, Angus, and his wife Hesther, dau. of Robert Conyers, a poulterer in Westminster, London, born 21 Mar. bapt. 4 Apr. 1819. [E]

STURROCK, THOMAS, son of Thomas Sturrock and his wife Lanceman, born 2 Aug. bapt. 8 Aug. 1813. [S]

STURROCK, WILLIAM, a merchant, church member, 1777, 1781.
[DCA.GD/EC/D10/1/2][S]

STURROCK, WILLIAM, son of David Sturrock, a baker, born in Monikie, Angus, and his wife Hesther, dau. of Robert Conyers, a poulterer in Westminster, London, born 18 Jan. bapt. 9 Feb. 1817. [E]

SUTHERLAND, ALEXANDER, born 16 Jan. bapt. 1 Feb 1824, 4th son of George Sutherland, born in Raffan, Banffshire, a labourer in Broughty Ferry, Angus, and Mary, dau. of John Swinney, a shoemaker in Gloucester, Engl.

SUTHERLAND, MARY NANCY, dau. of Alexander Sutherland and Elizabeth Wemyss, born 9 May 1812, bapt. 9 May 1813. [S]

SUTHERLAND, NANCY, dau. of Andrew Sutherland, a Sergeant of the 79th Regiment and his wife Elizabeth, born 4 June, bapt. 7 July 1811. [S]

SWAN, MARY, dau. of William Swan and Janet Clarke, born 21 Aug. bapt. 1 Sept. 1811. [S]

SYM, JAMES, son of John Sym and Ellen Peebles, born 28 June 1814, bapt. 13 Aug. 1815. [S]

SYME, WILLIAM, son of Alexander Syme and Elizabeth Hardie, born 20 July bapt. 7 Aug 1814. [S]

SYMMERS, ADAM, and his wife, members of the Scottish Episcopalian Church, Castle Street, Dundee, 1824. [DCA.GD.EC.D10.1/3]

SYMSON Mr, senior a vestryman, St Paul's, Dundee, 1836. [DCA.GD.EC.D10.1/3]

SYMSON Mr, junior, a vestryman, St Paul's, Dundee, 1836. [DCA.GD.EC.D10.1/3]t

TALBOT, MARIA, born 5 Feb., bapt. 20 Feb. 1827, dau. of Maria Talbot dau. of Thomas Talbot a pensioner of the Staff Corps and a tailor in Dundee. [E]

TALBOT, THOMAS INKSON, born 30 Mar, bapt. 13 June 1828, dau. of Maria Talbot, dau. of Thomas Talbot a pensioner of the Staff Corps and a tailor in Dundee. [E]

TASKER, JAMES, son of William Tasker, a smith in Cottarton of Craigie, Angus, bapt. 4 Sept 1725. [BN]

TAYLOR, ANN LEONORA, 1st dau. of John Butt Taylor, the surgeon of the 25th Regiment of Foot, born in Southwark, Surrey, England, and his wife Ann Guthrey, dau of Andrew Guthrey, born in Inniskilling, County Fermanagh, Ireland, was born 25 Feb 1809, bapt. 3 March 1809. [E]

TAYLOR, JAMES, member of the QEC, 1811. [DCA:GD/EC/D10/1/1]

TAYLOR, JAMES, member of the QEC, 1811. [DCA:GD/EC/D10/1/1]

TAYLOR, MARY ANN, born 9 May, bapt. 18 May 1825, 1st dau. of William Taylor, pensioner of the 71st Regiment of Foot, born in Banffshire, and his wife Catherine, daughter of James MacDougall, a shoemaker at Witchknowe, Dundee. [E]

TAYLOR, THOMAS, church member, 1743. [DCA.GD/EC/DIO/2/1; 2/3]

TAYLOR, Miss, member of the QEC, 1776. [DCA:GD/EC/D10/1/1]

TEASDALE, JOHN, Qualified Chapel minister, from 1781 until 1785. [DCA:GD/EC/D10/1/1]

TEVINDEALL, THOMAS, pensioner, 1739. [DCA.GD/EC/DIO/2/1]

THAIN, PATRICK, pensioner, 1739. [DCA.GD/EC/DIO/2/1]

THENEA (?), ANNE THOMPSON, dau of William Thenea (?) and his wife Ellen, born 8 July, bapt. 16 July 1815. [S]

THOMAS, JAMES, born 4 Dec. 1816, bapt. 24 June 1817, son of Henry Thomas, a weaver born in Wath, Yorkshire, England, and his wife Rosamond, daughter of Edmond Rivell in Newark, Nottinghamshire, England. [E]

THOMS, ALEXANDER, a merchant, church member, 1784. [DCA.GD/EC/D10/2/2][E]

THOMS, Miss, a member of the Scots Episcopal Chapel, Castle Street, Dundee, 1824. [DCA.GD.EC.D10.1/3]

THOM, WILLIAM, church member, 1764. [DCA.GD/EC/DIO/2/1]

THOMSON, EDWARD LIVINGSTONE, born 19 May, bapt. 22 May 1825, 2nd son of David Thomson, a writer, born in Ceres, Fife, and his wife Mary, daughter of Edward Livingstone, a jeweller in Dundee. [S]

THOMSON, JAMES, church member, 1781. [DCA.GD/EC/D10/1/2][S]

THOMPSON, JAMES, son of James Thompson an Elizabeth his wife, born 30 July, bapt. 18 Aug. 1812. [S]

THOMPSON, JOHN, son of John Thompson and Ellen Lindsay, born 1 Sept. bapt. 17 Sept. 1811. [S]

THOMSON, MARGARET JAMIE MACGRIGOR, born 25 Jan. bapt. 12 Apr. 1825, 2nd dau. of Robert Thompson, square-wright and cabinet-maker, born in Dundee, and his wife Ann, dau. of the late James Bruce, a wheel-wright in Bonnethill, Dundee. [E]

THOMSON, MARY SPEID PAUL, born 6 June, bapt. 18 June 1820, 2nd dau. of David Thomson, a writer, born in Ceres, Fife, and his wife Mary, dau. of Edward Livingstone, a jeweller in Dundee. [S]

THORNTON, BARBARA, church member, 1764. [DCA.GD/EC/DIO/2/1]

THOW, THOMAS, a bachelor in Dundee, and Christian Watson, a spinster in Dundee, were married in the house of James Watson, High Street, Dundee, on 7 Dec. 1831. [S]

TIBBETT, WILLIAM, 2nd son of John Tibbett, a Private of the 2nd Battalion of the 79th Regiment of Foot, born in Birmingham, Warwickshire, England, and his wife Sarah, dau. of James Govers, a painter in Longford, County Longford, Ireland, born 9 Apr. bapt. 14 Apr. 1811. [E]

TOMLINSON, JAMES, minister of the Qualified Chapel in Dundee, from 1769 until 1780. [DCA:GD/EC/D10/1/1] [DCA.GD/EC/D10/2/2][E]

TOPPING, ANN JANE, born 20 Feb., bapt. 7 June 1829, 1st dau. of James Topping, a weaver, born in Tullish, County Down, Ireland, and his wife Margaret, dau. of Major John Gordon of Drimmond, Inverend, Banffshire. [E]

TOSH, MARY, dau. of David Tosh and Elizabeth MacPherson, born 28 Jan. bapt. 16 Feb 1812. [S]

TOSH, THOMAS, a pensioner, 1746. [DCA.GD/C/D10/2/1]

TOSH, Mrs, widow of Alexander Tosh, a pensioner, 1742. [DCA.GD/EC/D10/2/1]

TOWNS, JANE, dau. of John Towns and Janet Thompson born 22 Aug. 1814, bapt. 23 July 1815. [S]

TOWNS, JANE, born 19 Feb., bapt. 5 Mar. 1826, 1st dau. of David Towns, a flax dresser, born in Brechin, Angus, and his wife Charlotte, dau. of the late Joseph Choice, a wright in Ballimeny, County Antrim, Ireland. [E]

TOWNSLEY, ELIZABETH, 4th dau of Andrew Townsley labourer, born in Inverness, and his wife Eleanor, dau of John MacDonald in Dingwall, Easter Ross, born 17 Aug. bapt. 11 Sept. 1814. [E]

TOWSON, JOHN, son of John Towson, a gauger in Dundee, was bapt. 23 Aug.1726. [BN]

TULLIDEPH, Dr, 1757. [DCA.GD/EC/D10/2/2][E]

TUTIN, MARGARET, a spinster in Liff, Angus, and Joseph Lawton Walker, a bachelor in Dundee, at the house of Rev. H. Horsley in Dundee, 24 Nov 1830. [S]

TWIDDLE, JEAN, a spinster in Dundee, married Peter Cabell, a weaver in Dundee, a bachelor, at the house of Mrs Addison, High Street, Dundee, on 21 June 1818. [S]

URQUHART, CHARLES, a member of the Scots Episcopal Chapel, Castle Street, Dundee, 1824. [DCA.GD.EC.D10.1/3]

URQUHART, CHRISTIAN, born 4 July bapt. 17 Sep 1820, 1st dau of Alexander Urquhart, a tinsmith in Dundee, and his wife Elizabeth Nicholl, relict of the late Donald MacLachlan, a shoemaker in Blairgowrie, Perthshire, and dau. of James Nicholl, a farmer at Milnhill, Newtyle, Angus. [E]

URQUHART, ROBERTSON, a cork-cutter, and Margaret Jack, both of Dundee, were married there 24 Mar.1823. [E]

VALENTINE, JAMES, a mealmaker, church member, 1764, 1777. [DCA.GD/EC /DIO/1/2/][S]

VALENTINE, JOHN, church member, 1764. [DCA.GD/EC /DIO/2/1]

VAN LOON, BAREND SAMUEL, 1st son of Barend Van Loon, a master mariner of the Anna Maria, born in Zerrickzee, Zealand, the Netherlands, and his wife Hannah, dau. of Samuel Tugman of Queen's Square, London, born 23 Mar., bapt. 16 April 1812. [E]

VAN LOON, JACOMINA, 1st dau of Barend Van Loon, master mariner of the Anna Maria, born in Zerrickzee, Zealand, the Netherlands, and his wife Hannah, dau. of Samuel Tugman of Queen's Square, London, born 19 Apr. bapt. 5 May 1814. [E]

VIOLENT, Mrs, 1739. [DCA.GD/EC/DIO/2/1]

VOLUMN, NELLY, a pensioner aged 70 in 1818. [S][DCA.GD.EC.D10.1/2]

WADE, ELIZABETH BAXTER, dau of James Wade and Barbara his wife, born 24 May, bapt. 5 June 1813. [S]

WADE, MARY ANN BAXTER, dau. of James Wade and Barbara his wife, born 24 May, bapt. 5 June 1813. [S]

WADMAN, CATHERINE HUTCHINSON, dau. of David Wadman and Elizabeth Constable, born 26 Oct. bapt. 19 Nov 1815. [S]

WAID, Captain ANDREW, a vestryman of the QEC, 1789. [DCA:GD/EC/D10/1/1] [DCA.GD/EC/D10/2/2][E]

WALCH, ANN, dau. of William Walch, a Lieutenant of the 21st Regiment, and Anne his wife, born 6 Feb. bapt. 14 Feb 1812. [S]

WALKER, ALEXANDER, son of Thomas Walker and his wife Mary, born 14 Jan. bapt. 28 Jan. 1816. [S]

WALKER, GEORGE, session clerk, 1811. [E]

WALKER, JAMES, son of James Walker and Catherine Thom, born 2 Oct. bapt. 23 Oct. 1811. [S]

WALKER, JANET, dau. of Thomas Walker and Marian his wife, born 16 July, bapt. 25 July 1813. [S]

WALKER, JOSEPH LAWTON, a bachelor in Dundee, and Margaret Tutin, a spinster in Liff, Angus, were married at the house of Rev. H. Horsley in Dundee, 24 Nov, 1830. [S]

WALKER, MARGARET, a pensioner aged 77 in 1818. [S] [DCA.GD.EC.D10.1/2]

WALLACE, AGNES, born 7 July, bapt. 9 July 182-, dau. of Elizabeth Wallace, dau. of Alexander Wallace, a farmer in Lamberkin, Duplin, Perthshire. [E]

WALLACE, ANDREW, and Jane Pyot, both in Dundee, married 15 Mar. 1818. [E]

WALLACE, ELIZABETH GRAHAM, born 12 Mar., bap.13 Apr.1823, 4th dau. of Thomas Wallace, a travelling merchant, born in Belfast, Ireland, and his wife Janet, dau. of Charles Robinson, a flax-dresser in Moulin, Blair Atholl, Perthshire. [E]

WALLACE, ELIZABETH, a widow in Dundee, and John Wharton, a widower in Dundee, were married in the vestry of St Paul's, Castle Street, Dundee, 24 May 1833. [S]

WALLACE, JANE BARNS, dau of Samuel Wallace and Jane Livy, born 9 Nov. bapt. 12 Nov 1815. [S]

WALLACE, JOHN ROBERTSON CRAWFORD, born 7 June, bapt. 26 June 1825, 4th son of Thomas Wallace, a travelling merchant, born in Belfast, Ireland, and his wife Janet, dau. of Charles Robinson, a flax-dresser in Moulin, Blair Atholl, Perthshire. [E]

WALLACE, MARGARET, 3rd dau of John Wallace gardener at Fingask, Perthshire, born in Dunnichen, Angus, and his wife Mary, dau of John Marjoribanks, a dyer at Thornhill, Perthshire, born 12 Jan. bapt. 19 Feb. 1815. [E]

WALLACE, MARGARET, born 18 July, bapt. 6 Aug. 1826, 1st dau. of George Wallace, keeper of the Lunatic Asylum, born in Dundee, and his wife Helen, dau. of David Peckman, a tailor in Dundee. [E]

WALLACE, MARGARET, among the 'poor of St Paul's' 1830. [DCA.GD.EC.D10.1/3]

WALLACE, MARY, dau. of James Wallace and Elizabeth his wife, born 30 July, bapt. 21 Aug. 1814. [S]

WALLACE, MARY, a member of the Scots Episcopal Chapel, Castle Street, Dundee, 1824. [DCA.GD.EC.D10.1/3]

WALLACE, ROBERT, church member, 1764. [DCA.GD/EC/DIO/2/1]

WALLACE, WILLIAM CANT, born 16 June, bapt. 24 July 1825, 2nd son of William Wallace, a labourer, born in Perth, and his wife Magdalen, dau. of John Halle, a nailer in Perth. [E]

WALLS, DAVID, son of John Walls and Jane his wife, born 23 Sept, bapt. 19 Oct. 1813. [S]

WANLACE, JAMES, born 6 July, bapt. 25 July 1826, 1st son of James Wanlace, a hatter, born in Perth, and his wife Elizabeth, dau. of James Ferguson, a ships carpenter in Dundee. [E]

WANNAN, THOMAS, merchant, and Hannah Grubb, both in Dundee, were married 2 May 1821. [E]

WARREN, FREDERICK PELHAM, born 10 Dec. 1822, bapt. 6 Apr. 1823, 2nd son of Frederick Warren, Captain of the Royal Navy, born in St James parish, London, now resident in St Mary's, Strathmartin, Angus, and his wife Mary, dau of David Laird of Strathmartin, Admiral in the Royal Navy. [E]

WATSON, Sir ALEXANDER, church member, 1743. [a Jacobite in 1745] [DCA.GD/EC/DIO/2/1; 2/3]

WATSON, CLEMENTINA, a member of the Scots Episcopal Chapel, Castle Street, Dundee, 1824. [DCA.GD.EC.D10.1/3]

WATSON, DAVID, born 10 Apr, bapt. 21 Apr. 1825, 4th son of James Watson, a weaver and waiter in the Coffee Room, Dundee, born in Monikie, Angus, and his wife Ann, dau. of George Myles a sawyer in Dundee. [E]

WATSON, GEORGE BUCHAN, born 19 Dec. bapt. 27 Dec 1829, 6th son of James Watson, a weaver and waiter in the Coffee Room, Dundee, born in Monikie, Angus, and his wife Ann, dau. of George Myles a sawyer in Dundee. [E]

WATSON, HELEN, in Dundee, and Thomas Greig, a cotton printer in Bury, Lancashire, England, were married in the house of James Watson, Rosefield, Dundee, 6 Oct. 1834. [S]

WATSON, HENRY DRUMMOND, 4th son of David Watson, a cutler, born in Dundee, and his wife Margaret Reid, dau. of John Reid, a labourer, born in Neilston parish, Renfrewshire, born 23 Feb. bapt. 28 Feb. 1809. [E]

WATSON, ISABELLA, of the Scots Episcopal Church in Castle Street, Dundee, in 1824, 'among the poor of St Paul's, Dundee, in 1830'. [DCA.GD.EC.D10.1/3]

WATSON, JAMES, QEC vestryman, 1809. [E]

WATSON, JAMES, born 11 June, bapt. 20 June 1819, 1st son of James Watson, a weaver and waiter in the Coffee Room, Dundee, born in Monikie, Angus, and his wife Ann, dau. of George Myles a sawyer in Dundee. [E]

WATSON, JAMES, a vestryman, 1823/1830. [E] [DCA.GD.EC.D10.1/1/3]

WATSON, JESSIE, born 22 Aug., bapt. 18 Sep. 1825, 3rd dau. of John Watson a mariner. [E]

WATSON, MARGARET, 8th dau of David Watson, a cutler, born in Dundee, and his wife Margaret, dau. of John Reid in Neilston, Renfrewshire, born 4 April, bapt. 28 April 1811. [E]

WATSON, MARGARET, a spinster in Dundee, and Hugh Samson, a bachelor in Dundee, were married in the vestry of St Paul's, Castle Street, Dundee, 28 Mar. 1829. [S]

WATSON, PETER, 3rd son of James Watson, a merchant, born in Meigle Perthshire, and his wife Margaret, dau of Archibald Hardie, an innkeeper in Edinburgh, born 12 Sept, bapt. 24 Sept. 1809. [E]

WATSON, ROBERT, son of William Watson, maltman in Dundee, bapt. 23 Nov. 1722. [BN]

WATSON, ROBERT, vestryman of the English Chapel, 1808. [E]

WATSON, ROBERT BOWIE, born 5 May, bapt. 13 May 1821, 2nd son of James Watson, a weaver and waiter in the Coffee Room, Dundee, born in Monikie, Angus, and his wife Ann, dau. of George Myles sawyer in Dundee. [E]

WATSON, THOMAS MYLES, born 28 July, bapt. 5 Aug 1823, 5th son of James Watson, a weaver and waiter in the Coffee Room, Dundee, born in Monikie, Angus, and his wife Ann, dau. of George Myles a sawyer in Dundee. [E]

WATSON, Captain WILLIAM, treasurer, 1750; vestryman of the QEC 1757. [DCA:GD/EC/D10/1/1][DCA.GD/EC/D10/2/2]

WATSON, Miss, member of the QEC, 1776. [DCA:GD/EC/D10/1/1]

WATT, Mrs JOHN, member QEC, 1810. [DCA.GD/EC/D10/1/2]

WATT, MARGARET, a spinster in Dundee, and James Nicoll, bachelor in Dundee, were married in the house of Rev. H. Horsley, Magdalene Road, Dundee, 11 Mar. 1836. [S]

WATT, Mrs, a member of the Scots Episcopal Chapel, Castle Street, Dundee, 1824. [DCA.GD.EC.D10.1/3]

WAUGH, Mrs, pensioner, 1739. [DCA.GD/EC/DIO/2/1]

WEBSTER, ALEXANDER, son of Thomas Webster and Mary Mitchell, born 14 Sept bapt. 2 Oct 1814. [S]

WEBSTER, ANNE, dau. of John Webster and Margaret his wife, born 29 June, bapt. 14 July 1816. [S]

WEBSTER, ANN, a spinster in Dundee, and William Garrie, a Corporal of the 62nd Regiment, bachelor in Dundee, were married in the vestry of St Paul's, Castle Street, Dundee, on 22 Sep. 1825. [S]

WEBSTER, GEORGE, a merchant, church member, 1764, 1777. [DCA:GD/EC/D10/1/2][S]

WEBSTER, JAMES, son of James Webster and Margaret Cuthbert, born 12 May, bapt. 16 June 1816. [S]

WEBSTER, JEAN, church member, 1764. [DCA.GD/EC/DIO/2/1]

WEBSTER, JOHN, son of Thomas Webster and Elizabeth Mitchell, born 3 Feb. 1801, bapt. 13 Jan. 1813. [S]

WEBSTER, MARGARET, dau of John Webster and Margaret Douglas, born 21 Sept. 1811, bapt. 14 Jan. 1812. [S]

WEBSTER, THOMAS, a merchant, church member, 1784. [DCA.GD/EC/D10/2/2][E]

WEBSTER, WILLIAM, a merchant, church member, 1777, 1781. [DCA:GD/EC/D10/1/2][S]

WEBSTER, Mrs, church member, 1764. [DCA.GD/EC/DIO/2/1]

WEDDERBURN, ALEXANDER, of Wedderburn, vestryman of the QEC, 1781, 1784. [DCA:GD/EC/D10/1/1] [DCA.GD/EC/D10/2/2][E]

WEDDERBURN, Dr JOHN, in Dundee, 1727. [ECD]

WEDDERBURN, Sir JOHN, of Ballindean in Perthshire, a vestryman of the QEC, 1783, 1784. [A Jacobite in 1745.] [DCA:GD/EC/D10/1/1] [DCA.GD/EC/D10/2/2][E]

WEDDERBURN, MARGARET, dau. of John Wedderburn eldest son of the laird of Blackness, Angus, was bapt. 31 Aug. 1725, godfather was John Wedderburn MD in Dundee and godmother was the Lady Blackness. [BN]

WEDDERBURN, ROBERT, of Persie in Angus, a church member, in 1784. [DCA.GD/EC/D10/2/2][E]

WEDDERBURN, Lady, church member, 1764. [DCA.GD/EC/DIO/2/1]

WEIDMAN, Mr, (Dutch)(of the sugar house) vestryman and member QEC, 1776. [DCA:GD/EC/D10/1/1]

WEIGHTON, JAMES, son of James Weighton and Isabell, his wife, born 12 May, bapt. 10 Aug 1812. [S]

WEIGHTON, MARGARET, dau. of James Weighton and Janet Ferrier, born 15 Sept. bapt. 18 Sept. 1814. [S]

WEIR, WILLIAM RICHARD JOBSON, son of William Weir and Mary Ramsay, born 12 June, bapt 25 Sept 1814. [S]

WEMYSS, JANE, 1st dau. of William Wemyss of the Royal Navy, born in Dundee and his wife Margaret, born in Dundee dau of Alexander Sturrock, born 3 Oct, bapt 9 Oct 1808. [E]

WEMYSS, JOHN, church member, 1743. [DCA.GD/EC/DIO/2/1; 2/3]

WEMYSS, MARTHA, dau of William Wemyss and Margaret his wife, born 19 June, bapt 13 Aug 1815. [S]

WEST, MARGARET HOOD, dau of James West, an ostler, born in Pitmoog, Fife, and his wife Elizabeth, dau of Thomas Forgan in Wemyss, born 20 Nov, bapt 1 Dec 1811. [E]

WEST, WILLIAM FORGAN, 1st son of James West, an ostler, born in Pitmoue, Fife, and his wife Elizabeth, dau of Thomas Forgan in Wemyss, Fife, born 4 Sept, bapt 25 Sept 1814. [E]

WESTWOOD, WILLIAM, son of George Westwood and his wife Janet, born 28 Jan. 1816, bap. 7 Feb. 1817. [S]

WHARTON, JOHN, a widower in Dundee, and Elizabeth Wallace, a widow in Dundee, were married in the vestry of St Paul's, Castle Street, Dundee, 24 May 1833. [S]

WHITE, ALEXANDER, 1st son of Charles White, a Private of the Aberdeenshire Militia, born in Dundee, and his wife Alexandrina, dau. of Colin Macleod merchant in Edinburgh, born 2 Mar, bapt t 6 Mar 1814. [E]

WHYTE, ALEXANDER, junior, a member of the Scots Episcopal Chapel, Castle Street, Dundee, 1824.[DCA.GD.EC.D10.1/3]

WHYTE, ALEXANDER, senior, a member of the Scots Episcopal Chapel, Castle Street, 1824. Dundee. [DCA.GD.EC.D10.13]

WHYTT, DAVID, and Elspeth Simson, were married in Ferry Port on Craig, Fife, 25 Aug 1811. [E]

WHITE, ELIZA CREIGHTON, dau. of Alexander White and Jane Griggy, bapt 16 Dec 1811. [S]

WHYTE, ELIZABETH RATTRAY, dau. of Charles Whyte and Lecksy his wife, born 13 Dec. bapt. 29 Dec. 1816. [S]

WHITE, JAMES, born 1 Apr., bapt. 17 Apr. 1828, 1st son of Stephen White a wright, born in Montrose, Angus, and his wife Ann, dau. of Charles Kay, an inn-keeper in Brechin, Angus. [E]

WHITE, JANE, born 28 Nov., bapt. 10 Dec. 1825, 1st dau. of Stephen White, a wright, born in Montrose, Angus and his wife Ann, dau. of Charles Kay, an inn-keeper in Brechin, Angus. [E]

WHYTE, ROBERT, son of the late Charles Whyte, a merchant in Dundee, church member, 1739; 1743, 1750. [DCA.GD/EC/DIO/2/1; 2/3]

WHITE, ROBERT, church member, 1781. [DCA.GD/EC/D10/1/2][S]

WHITTON, JAMES, pensioner, 1739. [DCA.GD/EC/DIO/2/1]

WIGHTON, WILLIAM STUART, son of William Wighton and Betsey Stuart, born 5 Mar. bapt. 24 Sept. 1815. [S]

WILKIE, MARY, dau. of Robert Wilkie and Ann Lownie, born 14 Aug. 1815, bapT. 9 Feb. 1817. [S]

WILLIAMSON, JAMES, a bachelor in Dundee, married Elizabeth Daly, a widow in Dundee, were married at the house of Lieutenant General C. Mackenzie in Broughty Ferry, Angus, 31 Oct. 1821. [S]; and his wife, members of the Scots Episcopal Chapel, Castle Street, Dundee, 1824. [DCA.GD.EC.D10.1/3]

WILLIAMSON, WILLIAM, born 13 Oct., bapt. 1 Nov. 1828, 1st son of Robert Williamson, a shoemaker, born in Perth, and his wife Mary dau. of George Cluney, a carter in Perth. [E]

WILLIAMSON,........., from Berwick, Northumberland, England, was appointed organist of the QEC in 1777. [DCA:GD/EC/D10/1/1] [DCA.GD/EC/D10/2/2][E]

WILLISON, ANDREW, a writer, [lawyer], and Margaret Murray, both in Dundee, were married 19 Feb. 1827. [E]

WILLS, JOHN, a tailor in Dundee, 1727. [ECD]

WILSON, ALLEN, son William Wilson and Jane his wife, born 9 Jan. bapt 30 Jan. 1814. [S]

WILSON, DAVID, son of William Wilson and Jean his wife, born 1 Oct. bapt. 20 Oct. 1816. [S]

WILSON, MARY, dau of James Wilson and Jane his wife, born 17 June, bapt. 28 June 1812. [S]

WILSON, THOMAS, a merchant in Dundee, 1727. [ECD]

WILSON, WILLIAM, born 24 July, bapt. 6 Aug. 1826, 1st son of William Wilson, a mariner, born in Aberdeen, and his wife Margaret, dau. of James Pearson, a shipwright in Dundee. [E]

WINDER, AGNES, dau. of George Winder and Elizabeth his wife, born 12 Apr. bapt. 16 May 1812. [S]

WINDER, ROBERT, son of George Winder and Elizabeth his wife born 13 June, bapt. 17 July 1814. [S]

WINTER, WILLIAM, church member, 1743. [DCA.GD/EC/DIO/2/1]

WOOD, DAVID, born 22 Apr. bapt. 10 May 1829, 2nd son of William Wood, a flax dresser, born in Dumfries, and his wife Jane, dau. of William Mill, a tailor in Montrose, Angus. [E]

WOOD, HANNAH, born 23 Sept. bapt. 23 Nov. 1828, 6th dau. of George Wood, a weaver, born in Donaghady, County Tyrone, Ireland, and his wife Margaret, dau. of William Rogers a weaver in Donaghady. [E]

WOULDHAVE, MARGARET, 1st dau of Robert Wouldhave, a Royal Military Articifer, born in Darlington, Durham, England, and his wife Isabella, dau of James Rantawl in Sunderland, Durham, England, was born 22 Oct, bapt 14 Nov 1810. [E]

WRIGHT, CHARLOTTE, dau. of James Wright and Anne Lyon, born 6 Jan. bapt. 20 Feb. 1814. [S]

WRIGHT, ELIZABETH, dau. of Thomas Wright and Maissy Morrison, born 11 Nov. 1812, bapt. 24 Jan. 1813. [S]

WYNYARD, WILLIAM ROWLEY, a Lieutenant of the Royal Navy, a bachelor in Eccles, Berwickshire, and William (sic) Elizabeth Laird, spinster in Strathmartin, Angus, were married in the house of David Laird in St Mary's, Angus, 11 Feb. 1830. [S]

YEAMAN, AGNES, dau of James Yeaman in the parish of Mains, Angus, bapt. 6 July 1723. [BN]

YEAMAN, GEORGE, merchant, church memer, 1777. [DCA:GD/EC/D10/1/2][S]

YOUNG, DAVID, born 28 Sept., bapt. 12 Oct. 1823, 1st son of James Young, a clock and watch maker, born in Dundee, and his wife Helen, dau. of John Low, a master mariner in Dundee. [E]

YOUNG, JAMES, a surgeon, church member, 1746, 1750 [DCA.GD/EC/D10/2/1]

YEAMAN, JAMES, of Murie, Perthshire, vestryman of the QEC, 1781, 1784, member, 1810. [DCA:GD/EC/D10/1/1] [DCA.GD/EC/D10/2/2][E]

YEAMAN, Mrs MARY, church member, 1746. [DCA.GD/EC/D10/2/1]

YEAMAN, ROBERT, son of James Yeaman in the parish of Mains, Angus, was bapt. 12 Apr. 1726. [BN]

YOUNG, DAVID, born 23 Aug., bapt. 5 Sep. 1829, son of James Young, a clock and watch maker, born in Dundee, and his wife Helen, dau. of John Low, a master mariner in Dundee. [E]

YOUNG, HELEN, born 23 Aug., bapt. 5 Sep. 1829, 1st dau. of James Young, a clock and watch maker, born in Dundee, and his wife Helen, dau. of John Low, a master mariner in Dundee. [E]

YOUNG, JAMES, a watchmaker, and Helen Low, both in Dundee, were married 8 July 1822. [E]

YOUNG, WILLIAM, son of John Young and Marianne Read, born 19 Mar bapt. 3 Apr. 1814. [S]

YOUNGSTON, JOHN, member QEC, 1776. [DCA:GD/EC/D10/1/1]